THE CHECKMATE MACHINE

How Modern Smart Tech Ruins Everything

Dave Cullen

I would like to thank my loyal subscribers across social media for your years of viewership, support and engagement. I salute you.

CONTENTS

INTRODUCTION

For several years now, I've railed against the concept of an entirely cashless society. There have been a few notable IT outages in recent memory, which have clearly illustrated the danger of over-reliance on IT infrastructure. Such outages can have severe impacts on financial systems, airlines, retail, and other industries. I think such incidents highlight the potential pitfalls of living in a heavily digitised world.

The effects of such outages manifest quickly and can impact wide sections of society. I recall one global outage that caused the local shops in my hometown to be unable to process card payments for a day. Of course, this wouldn't be an issue for cash purchases and only further serves to underline the importance of keeping cash in circulation.

This is why I believe it is essential that the very idea of a cashless society must be resisted. Cash provides not only financial freedom but also anonymity. Two things that tyrannical governments hate. Now, by no means am I suggesting that we, here in the Western World, are living under tyrannical governments. Pfft! What a crazy notion. As you're well aware, the governments of Western countries love their citizens and want nothing more than to uphold their individual human rights and freedoms. Right guys? Guys?

But... hypothetically, if an authoritarian regime did wish to subjugate its people, one means by which they could do this is through tighter control of the monetary system. This would come in the form of increasing limitations and restrictions placed on cash purchases. It would be an attempt to ween the public away from cash entirely.

Over the years, I've discussed the perils of an exclusively digital currency and how it could potentially force the public to surrender their privacy and consumer choice. Many people see digital currency as a natural progression of paper money being used less and less. More people tap to pay for things these days using their debit cards or some kind of banking app on their smartphones. Are such systems gradually training the public to give up on paper money? But what happens when there's another major IT outage, and this time, there's no cash? Cash would have been made completely obsolete and no longer considered to be legal tender. So, this could grind society to a halt. No one would be able to buy anything. Online and offline transactions would be impossible until the issue was resolved.

This underscores the vulnerabilities and potential technological bottlenecks created by such smart tech.

Furthermore, the main issue I have with digital currencies is that they are not going to work the way our current fiat currencies do. The digital currencies of tomorrow are designed with a key feature in mind: programmability.

A programmable digital currency is a very different

animal from using a fiat currency. Hypothetically, the digital money in your digital wallet could be programmed to operate in particular ways.

Imagine a scenario where you attempt to purchase a couple of beef steaks in your local supermarket. You go to the checkout and attempt to tap to pay for them. But the transaction is denied because you're told by some app on your phone that you've purchased too much meat this month. You're then offered a list of non-meat-based alternative foods instead.

It doesn't matter how much money you have in your bank account, a simple and small purchase could be denied by your government-controlled digital money for whatever reason they see fit.

You go to the petrol station and fill up your car with petrol or diesel. You attempt to pay for it in the store, but your purchase is declined because your personal carbon emissions app tells you that you've reached your allowance of fuel for the month. I guess you'll have to take public transport.

If you're deemed to have purchased too many items for your home that are deemed luxury or nonessential, you might have your purchasing ability throttled on a daily or weekly basis for some time. If you're deemed to have travelled too far around the country or flown too often around the world and produced too much carbon, then you might also face a similar penalty.

Digital money can not only be programmed to allow you to spend your money on certain items from certain places, but it can even go bad after a certain time. Digital money can be programmed to only be usable within a given period. Imagine receiving a social welfare or paycheck that can only be spent within thirty days.

This could mean that you would never be able to accumulate wealth. The amount of money allowed in your bank account could be capped at a certain level. This is rationing. This is control. This is the reduction of your money into being little more than digital gift vouchers.

Potentially, if a tyrannical government wished to punish an individual or restrict their movement, they could program that person's digital money to operate only within a certain radius from their home.

They could place severe limitations on their purchasing ability or simply switch their wallet off until they discontinue their political activism. Compliance could be forced upon a person or persons using digital financial controls and disincentives.

This could easily be applied to a person's online speech. We've witnessed increasing levels of censorship on social media platforms in the past ten years. But there have also been calls by politicians of Western governments to regulate these platforms further.

Back in 2016, I said that if you wanted to know what the future laws of your country would be when it came to freedom of speech, just take a look at the nebulous and Orwellian hate speech policies and community guidelines of most big social networks. Sure enough, governments across Europe continue to push for the implementation and imposition of laws that criminalise speech.

An individual deemed guilty of spreading content that isn't to the liking of the big mommy and daddy government could also face restrictions on their digital money.

As I've mentioned, with digital currencies, consumer behaviours can be nudged away from buying certain items and towards others. Few people would argue against the idea that we are increasingly living in a nanny state. Government overreach and bureaucracy are widespread these days. However, the potential for a truly dystopian nanny state is a genuine possibility with digital currencies.

Picture this. Some new glossy report is published by some moral busybody arm of the state or some "expert" think tank about how people are consuming too much alcohol. It's possible that the government could limit the number of alcoholic beverages a person can buy from a pub or off-licence.

The issue that people need to understand is that such invasive government overreach will always be sold to the public under the guise of safety and the "greater good."

There are people in our society today who have become accustomed to the state being an almost parental figure in their lives from the cradle to the grave. They see government as a necessary and (mostly) benevolent force in their lives. These people will see such social controls as in the public's best interest and a necessary form of progress.

I haven't even mentioned how your hypothetical tyrannical government would have the capability of viewing every one of your financial transactions with a digital currency. They could see everything you ever buy.

I've grown increasingly worried by the pervasiveness and power of modern consumer technology and the speed by which it has transformed our society. We haven't even stopped to consider the negative effects of it.

Touch-screen smartphones exploded onto the scene towards the end of the first decades of the 21st century. Within a few short years, smartphone adoption grew exponentially and soon became a normal part of everyday life. Have we ever really reflected on whether it's a good thing that we're carrying such powerful

Internet-connected, portable computing devices with us everywhere we go?

Smartphones are highly addictive things, made all the more addictive by the nature of some of the apps we use on them. Popular social media apps were designed with the intention of delivering user dopamine hits using their notification system.

The instantaneous access to unlimited amounts of content and information, along with the intrusive nature of the devices themselves, means that we have developed a symbiotic relationship with them.

The only way we could become any closer to these devices would be if they were physically embedded inside our bodies. This obviously leads to inevitable sci-fi predictions about how far down the technology slippery slope we might slide.

Elon Musk is working on developing a brain-computer interface with his Neuralink neurotechnology company. A truly disturbing notion, in my opinion.

Already, big tech companies know far too much about us. Imagine consenting to having a computer installed in your brain. Imagine how much worse our already unhealthy relationship with technology could become. Transhumanism is a topic I will discuss later in this book.

But this is the central problem of the trap of convenience. There's an inevitability about the advancement of the progression of consumer technology. The user becomes so dependent on it because of the convenience and value it's added to their life that the next logical step is for a merger between human and machine. A nightmarish future I hope to never live long enough to witness.

At a personal level, I recognise that there's a huge irony for me to talk in this manner. I was a technology journalist for many years. I reviewed laptops, smartphones, tablets, PCs, Macs, you name it. I eagerly kept up with all of the latest trends in consumer technology. I loved my gadgets and couldn't wait for the cool new thing to hit the market. I was a proper geek. But as time passed, I began to become increasingly concerned about the negative effects of these technologies.

The widespread adoption of mobile phones and then, later, smartphones, an age of Internet-connected devices, where the user has unlimited access to the Internet, everywhere they go. I've railed for many years about smartphone addiction and the anti-social effects of such devices.

I've also spoken out about how smart tech solutions are continuously sold with arguments about convenience and efficiency. Naturally, the more convenient and streamlined a system becomes, the more attractive it becomes to the end user. Adoption spreads quickly. The system becomes popular and ubiquitous, and then the old way of doing things is gradually phased out and retired.

Imagine there was another major global IT outage, and it affected the travel industry once again. Millions of travellers could be unable to fly on a plane or travel on a train because some QR code ticketing system doesn't work on their phones. But if the airline or train company still made use of traditional analogue ticketing systems (at least as an emergency backup) and good old-fashioned cash, this wouldn't be an issue.

What's become apparent is that the convenience of modern technology typically comes with some kind of trade-off. Sure your connected home smart speaker is certainly convenient. You can set alarms and reminders and ask them about the weather and general knowledge, or play your favourite music. But it comes with the drawback of being effectively a listening device. Your private conversations are potentially being eavesdropped on.

As I mentioned, I was a tech journalist for several years. Keeping up with the latest gadgets from Silicon Valley was the name of the game. But at a certain point, I grew weary of the increased computer and smartphone screen time in my life.

I was tired of the dominant force smart technology had become on a day-to-day basis. I yearned to be less connected to the online world and more present in reality.

I began to look around me and became increasingly aware that far too many people's eyes and attention spans were captured by their devices. Heads down, mesmerised by their screens as if hypnotised under a magical spell. I didn't want to be part of this.

How many times have you found yourself in a restaurant, pub, or other social setting, and you see a couple sitting together but not talking to each other? They're silent and glued to their phones. Ironically, they're probably making use of "social" media while treating each other in a completely anti-social manner. They're more connected to a person who could be on the other side of the world than the person sitting right in front of them.

Similarly, I've often witnessed an entire family in a restaurant all lost in their devices. Parents and children sitting together, not speaking. Just mindlessly tapping, scrolling, and swiping. It's highly disturbing how quickly this phenomenon gripped so many people.

I want to make it clear that I am not against the benefits that modern consumer smart tech has given us. High-speed Internet connections and data transfer capabilities, HD and 4K videos, video calls, instant messages services, incredibly high-resolution smartphone cameras, ride-sharing apps, mapping and satellite navigation systems, and near-field communication tech, to name but a few incredibly powerful and genuinely beneficial recent advancements.

So, why am I so uncomfortable with all of these smart devices and Internet of Things appliances? For one thing, I don't like how such a significant amount of our day-to-day activities and lifestyle are conducted through a smartphone.

Smart tech is intruding upon domains of our lives where it was never previously needed. I don't like the paranoid feeling that my handset is listening to and potentially watching me. Why is it that every once in a while, an advertisement pops up on screen in my social media feed for something I was talking about earlier?

I could be having a face-to-face conversation with someone about some consumer item I'm looking to buy, and then later that day, advertisements for that very specific item start appearing on my social media. This is quite common, and many people report experiencing this very same phenomenon. This cannot be a coincidence.

There was a time when I stopped using a smartphone and downgraded to a basic dumb phone. But for business purposes, it became necessary to go back to a smartphone.

Many people like the level of convenience this technology has given us a little too much, to the point where they become lazy. Business associates, clients, and contractors often make use of popular social networking apps, and if you're not present on those apps, you're practically invisible to them. Having a presence in some of these services becomes a frustrating requirement.

Furthermore, the Internet itself used to be an unparalleled research tool, and it still is, but I have to ask if it's quite as good as it used to be, given the increasing levels of censorship online. There's more information management and moderation than ever before. Whoever controls the Internet controls the free passage of information and will control people's perception of reality, the past, and the future.

In addition, with the proliferation of artificial intelligence content across the web, we have to be increasingly concerned about the potential for manipulation of news and information. Rest assured, I will drive further on the topic of AI later in the book.

Technology should simply be a tool to improve, enhance, and simplify a person's life, liberating us from the arduous nature of laborious work. But smartphones, Internet-connected devices, and apps actually feel more like they're sucking our time and attention and doing so while learning a great deal about us.

Perhaps we're reaching a point where we need to reconsider our relationship with these technologies and consider just how beneficial they really are.

CHAPTER ONE

Some time ago, I was in the supermarket. I brought my groceries to the checkout counter; they were scanned by the lady behind the counter. I then proceeded to try to pay for them, foolishly using my debit card rather than good old-fashioned cash. The card was declined. So, I tried again. Declined once more. Hmm…

This wasn't the first time this had happened. I've made this silly mistake more than once. I checked my text messages on my phone and discovered the source of the problem. I had neglected to reply to a particular text that my bank had sent me. I had made an online purchase the previous day, and they sent me a text requesting me to verify the purchase within a few hours with either a Y for yes or an N for no.

Typically, when banks text you after you've made an online purchase, the texts are usually just a confirmation message stating that the purchase has been made. No further action is required by you, the purchaser. But every once in a while, they send a text that requires you to reply to them within a set period of time, or else they'll place a block on your debit card. This is done to prevent fraud. If the bank doesn't receive confirmation from you that you made that particular purchase within the allotted time, your card won't work until you contact them.

This was my fault for not fully reading the text message when I received it and for just presuming it was one of those confirmation texts and not one of those text-us-back texts.

So, there I was, standing at the checkout counter like a moron, with all my items scanned and with no means of paying for them. I bagged the groceries, explained the situation to the nice lady behind the counter, and proceeded to engage in a fifteen-minute phone call with my bank, requesting them to remove the block on my card. Eventually, this was done, and I was able to pay for my items.

With a single click, our banks now have the ability to switch off our money and prevent us from buying things, including the essentials, such as food. Now, of course, this is technically my mistake. If I'd taken the time to open the bloody text and read it fully, I could have avoided this situation. But, at the same time, it could be argued that the bank should not be able to place a block on my debit card without first having a human being contact me directly with a phone call. Text messages are easily missed by accident.

Therefore, a bank simply texting a customer with an urgent message that they must reply to, lest their access to their money be switched off, is totally unacceptable. It's too big of an imposition on a person's life for it to be so inadequately communicated to them. I suppose this is a small complaint for me to make when stacked against the more serious issue of digital identities.

A digital Identity or digital ID is a concept that's been bandied about in recent years and something we're told will become the norm for every citizen in the future. We're told this is also supposed to be the solution to ending online anonymity on social media. Every user would need to log in to the Internet using a digital ID. So they would be unable to remain anonymous.

A digital identity works like a kind of virtual gateway that a person must make use of in order to access basic services. The ID would be located on a smartphone app and would be required to access not only your bank account (and digital money) but also to access healthcare, your digital passport, digital driver's licence, communications, the Internet, email and social media accounts, to access government services and more. In other words, the digital ID would be required to effectively take part in society.

Without a digital identity, a person would be unable to function in our modern world. They would be cut off from engaging in everyday life. Therefore, whatever hypothetical tyrannical government controls the digital identities and how they operate, controls the life of every individual. I suppose we should count ourselves lucky that our governments are so completely trustworthy and morally upstanding. Right guys? Guys?

There may be some people who see such a system as the fulfilment of some utopian sci-fi dream, but not me. I see this as a potential dystopian nightmare and a pathway to totalitarianism. The digital ID will be the means by which the smart cities of the future will operate and will permit unprecedented levels of government surveillance of a person's life, movements, and activities.

Unfortunately, I can see such systems becoming an inevitability unless there is significant public backlash. One means by which digital IDs will be sold to the masses is due to growing concerns about artificial intelligence.

Since about 2022, AI systems have suddenly exploded on the Internet. In just a short time, we've seen the proliferation of chatbots, language models, and AI art technologies. You can log into an AI system and use it like an advanced search engine. By typing a prompt, you can ask it to write you a story, revise a piece of text you've written, check your grammar and spelling, or write you a joke or poem. The results vary, but AI is becoming shockingly proficient at these activities. And then there's AI art.

From images to videos, AI can be instructed to create some incredible pieces of visual content. Although it lacks a certain soulfulness to it because it's not human-generated, AI art is a neat trick, achieved through synthesising and riffing on enormous amounts of pre-existing content and modifying it. I'll discuss AI art more in a later chapter.

Suffice it to say AI audio is equally impressive. It's possible to take large amounts of recordings of a person's voice and then get an AI to replicate it perfectly. So, you can write a piece of text and instruct an AI text-to-voice system to read it back to you in that person's voice. Again, it's impressive, but it's also shocking and highly creepy because this can be done to *anyone's* voice, living or dead. What's to stop a person from simulating someone's voice in this manner and then fooling one of their friends or family members over the phone?

I shouldn't need to elaborate on how such technology in the wrong hands could be used for extremely unethical and immoral purposes. This AI tech could easily be used to defame a person, by making it sound like a person has said something they haven't. The same goes for AI-generated images and videos.

Deepfake video footage could be created that could make it appear as if someone has done something illegal. From a legal perspective, defamation through AI-generated content in this manner could open up a rather ugly Pandora's box. Faking a person's identity online in this manner could also enable the fraudster to commit financial fraud.

In addition, AI videos and images could also be used to create fake people. These AI-created virtual people could create their social media profiles. As AI video and audio continue to advance and become more convincing, I think it's inevitable that this content will spread across social media like wildfire.

AI-generated scams and identity theft could become a major global crisis. As a result, a solution will likely be sought to resolve this headache. That solution might very well be the rollout of the digital identity system.

I could see the digital ID becoming mandatory to access the Internet so that everything a person posts online can be verified as coming from them. It would be the means by which their digital footprint can be tracked and confirmed. A person's online posts and content could be digitally watermarked.

In addition, with the introduction of the digital ID, it would not be possible to login to the Internet without one. This means that the fraudsters and scammers would need to make use of a digital ID also. So, everything they post can be traced back to them. Their online activity could be recorded through the blockchain also. Sounds like an ideal solution to the problem, right? Possibly not.

Ultimately, I believe the issue is that the digital ID becomes another potential bottleneck or Internet kill switch that a tyrannical government could flip if they wish to penalise a political opponent. Disabling a person's digital ID effectively cuts them off from society and ostracises them. The digital ID enables a dangerous level of centralisation of power, connecting everyone into a tightly controlled network.

In a world with a digital ID, it becomes practically impossible to engage in wider society without one. So, effectively, your citizenship is contingent on smart technology. We have to ask ourselves, do we want to live in a world where we're required to exist as digital citizens or e-citizens? Why should such advanced technology be the price of taking part in society? Should every individual not have the right to be a free and sovereign citizen without the need for such technology?

Digital Identity creates a scenario whereby the government grants or denies a person their basic human rights, entitlements, and freedoms by permitting a situation to arise whereby digital ID becomes necessary in the first place. But our rights and freedoms are supposed to be inalienable; they do not come from the government. They are, therefore, never supposed to be in a position to deny them. To do so is a violation of our God-given personal sovereignty and self-determination.

I think the fact that we've been collectively sleepwalking into this potential dystopian nightmare shows us the effect of the moral and spiritual decay that has descended upon our society. The state and big government have attempted to fill the void in the decline of strong institutions, civic society, religion, and self-reliant, close-knit communities. And the role of smart technology is changing. It's becoming less about offering value and convenience and more about enabling the creation of an authoritarian-based smart society where smart city panopticons are possible.

Perhaps this could explain why smartphones and social media have become such a significant presence in people's lives. The meaningful real-world human connections that were so common in past decades are being replaced by virtual relationships and intangible, shallow, digital bonds.

Ultimately, I think smart city life is antithetical to human flourishing because it only further entangles a person in a digital control grid. And I think smart cities are doomed to fail because they cannot fulfil a deeper human need within all of us. Smart cities basically reduce life to a relationship with the state and a life of meaningless consumption, where we're basically seeking permission from authorities to do what we want.

In this respect, modern tech is becoming less of a useful tool for our own benefit and more of a useful tool for the benefit of powerful corporations and governments. It's empowering them and not us.

I want to make it clear that I'm not a Luddite. I'm not against technology, but the breathtaking pace of the IT revolution of the late 20th century and the rise of big tech consumerism of the 21st century has resulted in a radical social transformation. It's a transformation that has reshaped the very fabric of life on a global scale without any real consideration for the consequences, both short and long-term.

In the latter half of my career as a technology journalist, I grew less interested in what modern smart technology could do *for* us and more concerned with what it was doing *to* us.

A smart city, married with some kind of ghoulish transhumanism, appears to be the ultimate endpoint of the journey we appear to be on technologically. Perhaps outside the smart cities will be a world that resembles an unregulated, wild West. Those of us who refuse to live in the smart cities will be forced to fend for ourselves and adapt to a simple, slower life of self-reliance and self-sufficiency off-grid.

And what would be the harm in admitting we've advanced too far, too fast, and that a technological regression was in order? The level of man's technology does not and has never determined his happiness or fulfilment, after all. Would a regression to the early 1990s or 1980s level of technology really be so bad? Could we go back to living without the Internet? Maybe that sounds ridiculous, but by comparison to where we might be headed in the future, I think it sounds preferable, maybe even ideal.

CHAPTER TWO

I've talked in some of my videos about the importance of retaining physical media like DVDs, Blu-ray, and also paperback and hardback books. There are several reasons for this. Digital content and records can easily be altered. Non-physical books and films can be modified and updated to align with the current sensibilities of our time.

Let's imagine some moral busybody decides that a classical work of fiction is "offensive" in some way or contains "problematic" material, words, or ideas. They could campaign to have the work modified, and the words changed. How truly Orwellian.

I find this kind of thing alarming, but also an act of cultural vandalism, and digital versions of books especially are enabling this. The arrogant idea that people of today believe modern sensibilities can be applied retroactively to classical works and that this somehow improves them is truly disturbing. I believe this kind of thing is a violation of the author's intellectual property. A book is a product of a particular time and a historical moment and should be allowed to reflect that period. Warts and all.

It's not particularly sophisticated in our culture if we're not able to accept and understand the cultural context of a particular period of time. But above all, it is a person's work, it's their creation, and no one, no institution or entity has the right to modify that decades later in order to bring it in line with contemporary thinking.

Why must past works be updated to reflect our society's changing morality? This isn't even addressing the fact that the moral standards of today are not fit to shine the shoes of the moral standards of decades past. So, when it comes to classic books, it's important to have copies of the original works when they were first published because you never know when the politically correct brigade will advocate for them to be altered. And who knows how much further such alterations could go.

Might we also see old films and TV shows changed, possibly using AI to alter dialogue or storylines deemed problematic or offensive? AI could be employed to seamlessly modify both audio and visual aspects of a movie in order to remove certain "offensive" words, stories, characters, or scenes. Dialogue can be manipulated, or lines can be added or removed. This can all be done seamlessly, whereby a person watching the film for the first time would never have known it had been modified. Material considered offensive can be changed, and a new ideological bias can be added to the story.

It's also worth asking the question, could AI tools even insert modern political agendas and ideology into such older films? Now, this isn't an issue if you've got a copy of the original film or TV show on DVD or Blu-ray. It only becomes an issue when a new version of the film or TV show is released.

I'm not saying this is definitely going to happen, but I think we should watch this space because nothing would surprise me if it did happen.

Let's see how things go, but given the pervasive nature of politically correct social engineering and agendas in Hollywood, nothing would surprise me. If the power to accomplish such politically motivated digital vandalism were possible, would you be surprised if certain activists pushed for this?

Now, there's another reason I strongly believe in having a collection of physical media, and that's because of streaming services. If films and TV shows are altered in the future in the way I've described, these altered versions will make their way to streaming services first. But also, certain titles can disappear from streaming services for various reasons, such as licensing or because the film or TV show is no longer popular, or it could be removed for cancel culture reasons. Whatever the reason, it's good to be prepared.

If a streaming service goes out of business, what then? If you've exclusively been using streaming to watch your favourite content, then you've now got no way of watching it outside of buying it on DVD or Blu-ray. And the same goes for music.

I've always preferred to have a physical copy of my media rather than rely on what is basically the potential flakiness of the cloud. This is not just because content can be removed at any time for any reason, including by the original artist or commercial rights holder, but you also have to contend with what happens when you have no Internet access.

When it comes to placing everything into the cloud, relying entirely on streaming services raises questions of whether you actually own something. Subscription services grant you access to something you once had in your possession, be it on a CD, a DVD, a Blu-ray, an SD card, a flash drive, or a hard drive.

Physical media becomes essential to ensure that the entertainment you love is preserved and to avoid it being removed or, as I say, being altered in some manner in the future. But hopefully, such a worst-case scenario won't occur. Having a massive archive of content backed up on a hard drive is ideal but also just extremely prudent.

I think we're far too reliant on streaming services, whose back catalogue can change at any time. There's nothing permanent about paying an ongoing subscription model, so you have access to content no matter how convenient it may be.

Purchasing something and physically owning it permanently - be it in a physical media form like a disc or just as a file on a hard drive - gives peace of mind, and there's no longer any fee thereafter. It's yours, and that's that. And I find that far more preferable.

Ownership matters. I'm not interested in being a permanent renter of media. The issue is especially exasperated by DRM. Digital rights management.

If you purchase a book with DRM-enabled from an ebook store, you're not really purchasing the ebook itself. You're purchasing a licence to access the ebook. So, you don't really own the ebook in the first place. If the seller decides it no longer wishes to sell that book, your copy will disappear from your e-reader device.

This is especially true in the new economic model of subscription services for everything, where we are essentially renting things that we previously would just buy outright.

Streaming services may be cheaper in the short term, but they're far more expensive in the long term over several years, though they do offer us the convenience of access across multiple devices. Plus, we can watch or listen to content anywhere in the world, and the range of content is gargantuan. The key word here is convenience because consumers sacrifice ownership of property for the ease of access and the simplicity that these subscription systems offer.

Whether it's a music service or a library of films or TV shows, you have a nice, clean, and simple-to-use UI and search feature with a wide range of material available, and you don't have to store all of it on your device or computer. It's all in the cloud, but it also means you have very little control over what happens to it.

A streaming company can go out of business, or a studio can discontinue a particular song, TV show, film, or video game. The same goes for an e-book, if the content you've purchased is digital only, especially if it's in the cloud, your access to it can be basically shut off for a variety of reasons.

Perhaps you can no longer afford the monthly subscription fee, or the owner of the intellectual property wishes to retire it for any number of reasons. They may also decide to move their content to a rival streaming platform because they've signed an exclusive partnership with them. This is another irritating aspect of streaming systems. Your favourite content can be pulled from one service and transferred to another.

This is why having the original work is so very important, especially a version of it that you can physically hold in your possession, which means it's offline, disconnected from any system where it can be digitally replaced with an updated version.

Even putting aside the possibility that films or TV shows could be altered in this manner, becoming reliant on entirely virtual systems for storage of our entertainment is ill-advised.

I'm not saying you should discontinue using

streaming services entirely, but rather, a mix of the two is preferable. Streaming services can be a great way of discovering content, even old movies and shows, but you need the backup of physical media just in case.

Ultimately, the streaming model for entertainment media is very much about changing consumer expectations so that they are no longer concerned with the outright ownership of their content. This is something we can push back against by building up our archives of DVDs, Blu-rays, CDs, and books.

CHAPTER THREE

Talking to Strangers on the Bus in the 90s

In the 1990s, there was something I especially loved about being on public transport. When I was on the bus, I really enjoyed striking up conversations with total strangers. The cordial and friendly nature that Irish people are known for was very much present in those days. This was before mobile phones were ubiquitous and long before smartphones, of course. It was also a few years before Dublin City had become as cosmopolitan as it is today. So, social trust among the population was high, and everyone spoke English.

If you didn't want to chat with someone, you could just stare out the window, try to sleep, or read a book or a newspaper. Some young people had cassettes and later CD Walkmen, so they functioned much like phones do today, it was possible to escape from reality and disappear into your own world. But headphones and earphones weren't quite what they are today, and it was almost always possible to hear what the person was listening to. Their music could be a little too intrusive throughout your journey. You felt like telling them to turn it down a bit.

For the most part, people didn't have anything to do on the bus, so they engaged in conversation with strangers sitting near them or next to them, and the bus became a social setting and a kind of mini hub of the community. But just a few years later, everything changed with the advent of phones and smart devices.

Suddenly, all that banter and chit-chat was gone; most everyone was absorbed in their own virtual world, head down, buried in a touchscreen a million miles away. As a result, trying to strike up a conversation with a stranger is not only difficult but, in many cases, inadvisable given how jarring and odd it's become with the passage of time. Yes, it's still possible, and it does happen, but much less frequently to the point where it's no longer the norm, and most people don't want to be disturbed. They're more defensive now, and social trust is very low these days, so they might even feel a bit weirded out or threatened by you.

People have become much more remote, hostile, and suspicious, which is understandable given how our societies have radically changed, but it's nonetheless deeply saddening to witness.

I've spoken many times in the past about the negative social impact of smartphones as they drag us out of the moment and into endless distractions and shortened attention spans. The zombification of our nations and the isolating, atomising nature of being lost in one's own digital world. This small rectangular machine of plastic and glass continuously and intrusively pulls our focus away from reality and into the virtual, encouraging obsessive-compulsive checking of notifications, updates, news, and social media, and that provides unending entertainment, and visual stimulation.

My generation was the last to remember a time before such devices and, indeed, a time before the Internet itself. Can the youth of today even conceive of life before such pervasive technology? If they found themselves transported into the past, how challenging might it be for them to adapt to the slower pace of life? Being forced to be more present and no longer able to retreat into the fantasy worlds offered by their devices, which to them have become like an extra limb.

We forget how much less contactable people were before mobile phones. You had to rely on landlines and plans to meet someone had to be firmly made well in advance with an agreement as to where you would meet a person.

I've never believed in the ridiculous notion of socialising online, sitting alone on a computer or a device and speaking virtually to people is not socialising. This would have been obvious to people in the 90s. The level of self-isolation that technology has driven us to in the past two decades would be seen as abnormal and antisocial before the early 2000s.

The fact that smart devices offer people immediate communication and feedback, information at our fingertips, and constant connectivity can only contribute to a mindset of instant gratification and intellectual laziness. Perhaps even cognitive decline as people communicate over social media using fewer words and conversing in a less sophisticated manner.

I'm especially disturbed when I see young children on smartphones and tablets. I don't envy parents these days as these devices have become like pacifiers for their children who are addicted to playing games and being glued to their screens.

What the long-term effects of this are going to be, one can only speculate. But without a doubt, smartphone tech and internet-connected devices have had a shockingly transformative impact on society to the point where living life without these things has become practically impossible. And this is my frustration.

I remember that in 2002, I finally got my first mobile phone, and I was one of the last in my friend circle to do so after holding out for as long as I could. The latter half of the 90s and the early 2000s saw mobile phones suddenly become normal personal items.

But what was curious was the way life had been perfectly fine before mobile phones; people weren't clamouring for them, and no one cared much for the old brick handsets that were used only by the minority in the business class.

But suddenly, the Nokia 3210 emerged, and after that, all of these mobile phone manufacturers sprang up from nowhere, and it wasn't long before the vast majority of people, young and old, owned a mobile phone.

Go back to 1998, if you owned a mobile phone, you were in the minority, by 2003, if you *didn't* own one, you were in the minority. The pace of life changed as a result, and there was a sudden expectation of being always in communication reach.

The fact is, mobile phones were so incredibly powerful and invaluable that as soon as they became sufficiently streamlined and affordable, they were always going to become popular. They changed how people contacted each other, and their value and usefulness became immediately apparent. They were obviously useful in emergencies, and they enabled us to alter or amend our plans on the fly.

By not owning a mobile phone, you became stuck in the past by comparison, and your lifestyle felt outmoded.

Like I said, I was a holdout for a long time, everyone in college had a mobile phone except me, my parents bought me one in 2002. But before that, I was feeling at a disadvantage because I was still using payphones, which are now a relic of the past. And it wasn't like some kind of peer pressure or envy had caused people like myself to finally get a phone. It was because everyone else had gotten one, and they were now making plans and enjoying a new lifestyle with the benefit of having a phone.

If they were using their landline much less or not at all and primarily using their new mobile phone for communication, contacting them became extremely difficult without owning my own mobile.

Before mobile phones, phone calls were on landlines and usually quite long so that people could exchange all their stories and information that they had accumulated since the last time they spoke to that person.

Likewise, when planning a trip, a family dinner, drinks with friends, whatever it might be, and especially when it came to emergencies, mobile phones facilitated the exchange of information in a faster, more personal, and more convenient manner. Consequently, conversations didn't have to be super long. They could be continuous, several short calls throughout the day, you weren't hogging a single landline, and you no longer had that communications bottleneck anymore.

You also had SMS texts, so you could send short messages quickly and instantly. You could rearrange meeting points and dinner and drinks plans minutes before the event was due to take place. With texts, you could forward messages to multiple people, updating them with important information instantaneously. If you didn't have a mobile phone, you were unable to take part in any of this and were effectively, from a social perspective, alone out on an island by yourself. You were cut off from everyone else who had technologically evolved their means of communication.

When touchscreen smartphones hit the scene, the tech landscape changed dramatically. This kicked off another tech revolution with touchscreen-based devices exploding in popularity to the point where pretty much everyone owns one now.

Furthermore, the social pressure to get one was even greater given the level of communication apps and social media sites most people signed up to.

I still use text messages myself, but most people I know use some kind of messaging app service. Not being part of the latest social media network cuts you out of communication with so many people. We've reached a point now where it's very difficult not to have a smartphone, for example, an increasing number of banks, social networks, and other services require you to do two-factor authentication with your phone to access your account. It's essentially becoming mandatory to own a smartphone.

I'm sure there was someone thinking something very similar to me before the advent of the telephone and landlines in the home. What's shocking is how quickly technology radically alters the social fabric to the point where functioning without it becomes extremely challenging. You can try to opt out for a time, but if enough of the general population adopts a new transformative and disruptive communications technology in their daily lives, inevitably you find yourself being forced to follow suit before too long.

This is where I grow increasingly concerned when it comes to how our society normalises things, and within a generation, it's taken for granted and not questioned as if it couldn't be any other way. The same goes for social, political, moral, and ethical issues.

I don't want to see a situation in a few years where our smartphones become almost weaponised against us. Because the hypothetical smart city you live in will require you to own one, it'll have your digital ID, your digital wallet, your carbon score, etc. Your smartphone becomes the means by which you engage within the system. If enough people were to discontinue using these devices, such a system would become untenable.

No doubt, when you explain why you're against such intrusions into your privacy and personal liberty, some will respond by highlighting the benefits of such technology or by saying, "You're against progress," and "You can't live in the past."

These are the same kinds of replies some of us received when we first objected to the need for mobile phones in the early 2000s. So, becoming decoupled from these kinds of devices and systems is frankly crucial to extracting ourselves from that hypothetical control grid. Ultimately, people must weigh up the positives versus the negatives of smart tech and decide if the benefits are worth the potential hindrances and undesirable outcomes.

Finally, going all the way back to the point about talking to strangers on the bus in the 90s, I feel that technology has made a lot of our communication become much less personal. People are less likely to strike up a conversation in the real world with a stranger sitting right beside them than they are to message a faceless avatar on social media. Convenience has replaced a tangible and authentic quality that makes us social and, ultimately, human.

CHAPTER FOUR

As you're probably aware by now, AI is becoming incredibly powerful. There are these new text-to-video AI systems that can generate video from the prompts you write. Just describe what you want, and it'll go off and generate a video. And it's getting incredibly realistic to the point where it's becoming very difficult to tell the difference between reality and AI fantasy.

AI is learning, advancing, and becoming better all the time. It's a concern, if I'm honest, because I think we've opened a Pandora's box now, and I don't know where we go from here. Certainly, people have pointed to the benefits, Hollywood potentially being defunct and irrelevant. You wouldn't need to film anything anymore.

Actors may not be all that necessary. You might just have to shoot some scenes or use some actors for some minor reference purposes, perhaps, but for the most part, all the work of production crews and post-production crews won't be needed. And there's a lot of people who are celebrating this, understandably. I have no love for Hollywood in its current form. And people ask, Isn't this great? Soon, anyone will be able to make incredible films and visual art with just a few text commands. Maybe some reference footage, and bang! Build and edit your own film!

In the immediate term, this looks like an

imagination machine of near-infinite power where anything can be conceptualised and produced. Such technologies will enable extraordinary degrees of content creation. Some people have understandably pondered, "Isn't this like the birth of a new printing press? The ability for everyone to tell stories that previously couldn't be told?" Indeed, it is very possible that a new generation of AI-based filmmakers, people who previously had zero filmmaking skills, can now make films. Isn't this amazing?

Like I said, I have no love for Hollywood, but I do have a great deal of love for the art form of filmmaking and all of the skills that that entails. I actually think that we should consider where these AI systems will take us, not in the short term, not with respect to immediate novelty or entertainment purposes or the pure cool factor that will wear off in a matter of months, but more than that, in the long term, what will this do to us? What will such technology do to our culture?

I'm glad we've automated many laborious tasks. It's nice to have a washing machine and a tumble dryer. But in some industries, a lot of blue-collar manual labour work has already been made redundant, putting millions of people out of jobs and humans replaced with robots. And people are told just to reskill and go into a different field, preferably a white-collar field. Sit at a desk and enter stuff into spreadsheets. But that was just a retreat to a safe place until such time as white-collar jobs got the same treatment.

AI is not some cool new tool or innovation that is designed to make our lives easier or give us more free time. It's the very last step in the replacement of human beings in the labour market.

If human beings aren't needed for physical work and someday soon they won't be needed for mental work either, what purpose will human beings have? What meaning will they be able to derive from life? What function will we be able to assume? And I don't mean to ask this question from a purely economic, industrial, or mechanistic perspective.

We obviously shouldn't view human beings as little more than widgets or cogs in the economic engine of the labour market for the purposes of raising GDP per capita. I'm not talking about the utilitarian usefulness of a person as a taxable wage slave working for a corporation. I'm talking about the more philosophical aspect of... the meaning of life.

There has to be some kind of reason for being, some reason to get out of bed, some adversity or struggle for man to overcome, a feeling of fulfilment, and a sense of accomplishment in the process of putting food on the table.

Humanity, en mass, cannot become idle and sedentary. Sitting around, pushing buttons, and receiving money in the bank sounds easy, but perhaps not the best way of achieving a fulfilling life.

We, as a species, must be kept occupied with meaningful toil and not simply reduced to being domesticated animals in a zoo or a farm where all of our basic needs are supplied for and catered to by machines.

This sounds like what life might be like in a futuristic smart city surrounded by machines that would rob us of our usefulness. And now, with the advent of neural network AIs, it will be possible for even our cognitive labour to be automated, so what becomes of our quality of life?

Are we to simply be living in a virtual world existence where we engage only in hedonistic and frivolous pursuits, where we just watch entertainment all day until we die? Are we to merely exist within virtual worlds created and run by AI, which are designed to keep us somewhat satiated?

People think that AI will be used purely as a tool to help shortcut the creative process or to speed up cerebral labour, but I don't think this is the case. I liken it to when a chess computer program was finally developed that could beat the best chess masters forever. That was like a mini singularity, a threshold that had been crossed, where humans are no longer the masters of an activity they created. But now it appears as if we could be about to pass a far more serious threshold.

AI is going to get better and better and will eventually exceed human potential when it comes to all cerebral labour, including creativity.

So, for some time, humans will use AI to make art and write books and films using a few prompts, we will guide the AI and have it help us to make new and exciting stories. Until such time as the prompts themselves are no longer needed, and the AI will simply know us so well it will be able to produce more sophisticated and creative works of art, films, books, and games faster, more competently, and more frequently than human beings ever could.

You see, the very concept of AI is that more and more links in the creative chain become automated. Not just some of it, but most of it. Including the need for human involvement.

Where is this leading? Possibly to a generation of people who are unable to function without technology and advanced automated systems to run their lives. A class of people who don't even understand how the technology they use actually works. These would be infantilised people who would be easily controlled by a nefarious regime.

I fear that man's cognitive and creative capabilities will atrophy because these skills will have been outsourced to machines that can do it all better and infinitely faster. Look at many members of Gen Z; a lot of them cannot read cursive writing because of computers in schools, and the art and skill of cursive writing is no longer taught.

Will there be a future generation that cannot do very much for itself at all because it's all been farmed out to robots and artificial intelligence?

If human beings are no longer needed for their bodies or their minds, what will be left for them? Are we expected to sit all day with a VR headset scrolling, swiping, and watching content that a machine created for us? Are we to be living in virtual worlds created by machines until such time as the VR headset goes away and is replaced by a brain chip implant?

The AI has decades of human-created content to draw on and extrapolate from, which is what it's doing when it creates something. Paintings, photographs, videos, sound, music, blog posts, books, films, all of this consumed, understood, absorbed, And riffed on. All of it can be approximated, remixed and transformed into something new.

In the beginning, people will look upon AI's incredible creations with a mix of disbelief and shock at how amazingly believable these things are and how they look so real. And the wow factor, the cool factor, will eventually be replaced by a sinking, "uh oh" feeling. A realisation that our merciless technological advancement has gone too far and crossed a rubicon.

Humanity will have built a machine that has made us redundant and irrelevant. So, to people who say this is great, we can take on Hollywood. You're missing the point.

Forget about Hollywood. That should be the least of your concerns. The AI will eventually be able to take on *you*.

Do we want filmmaking, writing, editing, and storytelling skills to atrophy in the next generation because they no longer need those skills? The AI is handling it all for them.

Do we want a machine that can checkmate us not just in chess but in every area we as humans once dominated? It seems strange that humanity is moving intentionally in this direction. It's as if, on some unconscious level, we wish to be replaced by superior machine intelligence.

There have been plenty of science fiction stories that have offered stark warnings of the dangers of constructing an advanced, synthetic, machine-based life form. Its creation, much like AI today, is always heralded in the beginning as a beneficial new tool for humanity, a glorious dawn of a new and better world. But as always, the AI has other ideas.

The inevitable conflict arises where humanity is forced to fight for its own survival and primacy as the dominant intelligent life on the planet. It appears that science and technology are mirroring fiction once again.

The obvious question has to be asked: How is this defeated? How do we avoid the dumbing down of humanity? We have to step away from the machines. At some point, a technological regression becomes the only choice.

The Human Spark vs Artificial Intelligence

It seems, that in short order, audiences will be able to instruct an AI tool of some sort to generate more entertaining content for them, be it music, films, short clips, or interesting pieces of art.

We might reach a point in the future where maybe you want to read a new book. You have a general idea of the kind of book you're looking to read, maybe a who-done-it murder mystery based in London in 1930 with an interesting series of twists in the style of an Agatha Christie novel.

The AI will go off and quickly generate a novel for you, approximating and synthesising similar stories to produce something new but clearly based on books that have gone before in that genre.

The same will be true in live action whether you want the AI to generate a funny short clip or a full motion picture or television-length episode.

With a few prompts, you can describe the situations, the characters, and the basic outline, and off it goes to make it for you. New AI filmmakers and writers could write prompts and build a film scene by scene using AI tools; even the editing tools they use will employ AI.

So, this is obviously a recipe for unlimited content generation, and content is the key word here. Because since the advent of the internet and, in particular, social media and streaming services, there's an insatiable appetite for content, for stuff.

We often complain about a culture that is stupefied and quite docile, happily consuming and bingeing some streaming service every evening. Imagine combining an advanced AI with a streaming service.

It brings a whole new meaning to the term on-demand. Now, the streaming service can just generate new content on the fly for you, endlessly fulfilling the neuro-receptor dopamine addiction that mass media, smartphones, and social media have created in our culture.

The ubiquitous nature of an always-connected Internet culture, along with the pervasiveness of social media in our lives, has created this obsessive-compulsive need in people to check notifications, to seek updates on things of interest to them, the latest regular diet of content they enjoy, communications they receive, messages, whatever it is. Add to that other Internet-connected home products and wearables, and the human brain is just inundated with novelty, alerts, and attention-grabbing updates.

This was how social media apps, in particular, were designed. Right down to the swiping and pull-down menus and scrolling systems, which emulate the handle of a slot machine.

So, the reason I bring this up is to provide more context to the conversation because it's not just the effects that AI will have on our entertainment media, potentially putting screenwriters, filmmakers, and production crews out of work. Even making painters, writers, and musicians obsolete in some instances.

And, of course, making much white-collar work redundant. It's more than all of that. We have to consider the emergence of such an incredibly powerful AI content-creation tool in the context of the social media and on-demand media environment we live in.

There's already an enormous amount of low-quality content to consume rather than outright quality. It's basically a high noise to low signal ratio. Imagine how much worse the noise and poor-quality content becomes with the advent of AI-user-generated content.

How much screen time and social media use is in a young person's life these days? A young generation is growing up with their heads buried in smartphones, with all manner of distracting and engaging apps capturing their attention. They've grown up believing that this is all perfectly normal, their heads being filled on a daily basis with endless amounts of social media content and stuff. So, it's created this need for habitual visual stimulation and instant gratification.

Now imagine how much that can be satiated by an AI that can literally create anything you want. But the thing is, what the AI will do is largely derivative. Now, that doesn't seem to bother most people.

Look at the quality of films and TV shows coming out of Hollywood these days. It's simply copy and paste plots, cookie-cutter scripts, and stories. It's felt very assembly line, mass-produced for a long time.

So, if the masses have been acclimated to watching stock standard films and TV shows for many years, scripted fiction that just ticks the boxes in terms of basic delivery of novelty and lowest common denominator entertainment, then it stands to reason that AI will be used to create yet more low signal and high noise. More low-quality, quick-fix, fast-food escapism to satiate the appetite for new products.

Now, there is an upside to this, I believe. I think we'll enter a point, as Robert Meyer Burnett has described, where the currency of the future will be authenticity. And as a friend of mine pointed out recently when I spoke to him about this, AI cannot truly innovate and do unexpected things. So, it lacks the true God-given human spark of ingenuity and creativity.

After the AI magic trick has been done enough times, we take it for granted that we have an AI technology that can churn out infinite amounts of sub-standard, unimaginative, and derivative stuff. There will be a market for something different. Because although it's impressive to have such a powerful AI, the AI cannot produce original stuff that genuinely amazes. It can only make stuff that is essentially an approximation of what human beings can make.

So, although human beings can't compete with the speed of the content output of the AI, they can better it when it comes to artistic flair and imagination.

Moreover, the imperfect nature of human creation is what will be a key selling point of human-made entertainment and art in the future. Authenticity that cannot be faked.

As I've mentioned before, I fully expect that future films, music, books, etc, will carry a label on them to differentiate them from machine-made creations. A label that reads, "No AI was used in the creation of this work," akin to a label on food denoting that it is organic and not GMO.

There will be those who will continue to make films and music and write books in the way they always have, simply because they want to. They want to experience every stage of the creative process of an artistic work because they can. Because of the sense of satisfaction and accomplishment that it brings them.

There is no sense of accomplishment with inputting a series of prompts into an AI and having it spit out a generic superhero movie that titillates and placates for a period of two hours and is then forgotten. This is no better than the current dreck being pumped out by Hollywood.

An AI can make a love story but cannot make a labour of love, and the critical word is labour. People love to work on things in which they can see their artistic talent expressed. And the human soul cannot flourish in a future where this has been taken from us.

So, when you think of it, human-made art and filmmaking might actually go back to being an even more revered and respected profession because of the existence of AI. Because AI will make it rare and more niche, there will be all manner of AI-generated content, but none of that can be heralded or championed or contribute to the pantheon of artistic works throughout history.

There will be those who will value the merit of human industriousness and artistic craft. These people will have a more discerning palate and will be unsatisfied with the sameness and predictability of AI.

They will desire a more refined experience and will choose the human-made media. This human-made content will likely have to become more clever and inventive as a result of competing with AI media. But the only stumbling block will be, of course, money.

AI doesn't need any money whatsoever. Human films and TV shows will require funding as they will not be able to compete on a level playing field in this regard.

So, I still have hope that human creativity can endure because people will always want art with true soul and heart behind it. They will want to experience the unpredictable and innovative human touch in their entertainment.

But ultimately, we should never have touched this Pandora's box because we're now having to unnecessarily compete with a tool that should never have been invented.

There have been a few recent films over the past few years that can be categorised, in my opinion, as little more than content and not art. These are films that have absolutely zero creative merit and seem to be little more than the result of studio executives having corporate boardroom meetings and deciding to churn out a stock product based on a popular intellectual property.

Of course, that's technically true for even good films, too, but it just becomes so much more noticeable when the end product is a lifeless, generic, and formulaic paint-by-numbers snorefest. Something that feels more like a blatant tax write-off than a serious cinematic and creative, artistic effort.

This made-by-committee filmmaking has characterised many Hollywood franchise films and dull and dreary derivative standalone movies for some time now. You know, the kind where you walk out of the cinema asking, why was that even made, how did it get greenlit, let alone shot, post-produced, and released?

When streaming services became popular, they soon began to produce their own original films and TV series. They greenlit so many productions that there was a glut of material, too much to actually consume. And though there were plenty of great original series and films in there, a huge amount will be forgotten as nothing more than content, stuff, and filler.

How many decades worth of TV series exist now that will be discarded and forgotten in the din of mediocre productions that made no impact at the time and offer zero entertainment value for the future? As if they were created simply to meet consumer's insatiable appetites for the instant and endless gratification of having yet more products to consume.

Somewhere in the rush to make new products as fast as possible to satisfy this hunger, the importance of quality of storytelling, meaning, and artistic originality was lost. These films and TV shows will be remembered only for how low they set the bar and how much they detracted from the quality of their franchise.

I thought recently about how much worse this could become in the wake of AI-generated entertainment. Imagine the endless possibilities for more bland filler content that could be created by text-to-video artificial intelligence systems.

As the systems become more sophisticated, requiring only small amounts of reference images, audio, and video to work off of, it's inevitable that AI will contribute to producing unlimited amounts of new material.

Not all of it will be bad, of course. Some creative AI filmmakers will make some genuinely innovative and clever stuff. But with the sheer ease of use of the AI systems and ubiquity of the technology, there will no doubt be orders of magnitude more content creation than ever before, especially from indie filmmakers.

There will be so many more films produced using AI, which will streamline and accelerate the production process to the point where it will become impossible to keep up with.

Although some great stories can be told using this technology, by sheer weight of numbers, most of it will have to be rubbish. Very little of it can be good. So, high noise, low signal. Sifting through the noise becomes the challenge.

As for how this transforms Hollywood, that's an interesting topic to ponder. No doubt, for a while, there will be a blending of traditional and AI filmmaking techniques.

Films will be partially filmed and edited in the normal way and partially made using AI, and then, as AI advances, it might very well take over the entire process. Humans would only be needed for prompts and cleaning up in post-production.

Hollywood could save an enormous amount of money on production budgets by simply feeding its huge archive of films and TV shows into the machine. AI could riff and extrapolate on it, churning out more derivative content based on existing material.

The advantage Hollywood studios have is that they own the rights to the intellectual properties, the big franchises, and the characters. So, they can continue to make money making new franchise films via AI, but at a fraction of the cost.

Therefore, the profit margins will be huge. So too, will be the potential for more rubbish cookie-cutter content based on these IPs, with the art of filmmaking further reduced to synthesising and approximating what went before.

Suffice it to say that AI filmmaking has probably opened the door to many more mediocre productions with little to no real artistic merit.

But there will also be opportunities for indie filmmakers to really show what they're capable of and showcase their creativity and imagination.

CHAPTER FIVE

Musings on AI-Generated Vs. AI-Assisted Content

Legislation is still evolving when it comes to artificial intelligence. I'm specifically referring to content generated by AI. These are the distinctions between purely AI-generated content and content that is classified as AI-assisted. And it's an absolute grey area in some respects because AI tools are encroaching into applications more and more.

For example, certain graphic design applications are increasingly incorporating AI tools. Where once you might have to manually and painstakingly remove a background from a photograph in order to isolate a person in the foreground, now some AI tools will do this with a single click.

Over the next few years, you're likely going to see significantly more AI functionality in video editing applications also, allowing for more automation in workflow and previously laborious editing and video processing tasks.

I've already discussed how transformative AI could be for creative industries, but it's important to remember that AI-generated content cannot be copyrighted. As a result, it's considered public domain content.

AI-assisted content is a different matter, however. Technically, if you've created something and used AI to augment it or revise it in some way, that's ok. You still retain legal authorship of that content. You can copyright it. But sometimes, the definition of what is AI-assisted can be a bit unclear. As I'm not an expert on this matter, however, it is best to consult a legal authority on this.

For writing, AI language models can be a great way to help generate ideas or assist in detecting grammar, punctuation, and spelling mistakes. It can also help with editing, but it should never be used for actually writing something for you, assuming you want to actually be the owner of the content.

Personally, I don't think we should be outsourcing our creative abilities to a machine. Although AI can write very nice literary prose, it lacks the ability to generate original ideas because it can only really synthesise and riff on previously created works.

AI art generators can be great for assisting artists in coming up with simple mockups for their designs. It can assist them to create a preliminary visualization of the concept they have in their heads. But when it comes to actually creating that original piece of art, in order for it to truly be their own, the artist must create it from scratch themselves.

AI makes for a fantastic word-processing assistant, as I've mentioned. In fact, the advent of AI grammar detectors and spellcheckers only further serves to underline how poor conventional word processors have been for so long.

I find that some of the most popular word processors sometimes miss so many basic errors in a document, it's astounding. Augmenting a word processor with an AI assistant of some kind is extremely beneficial, so long as you're only using this to improve grammar, spelling, and punctuation and finding the odd duplicated or missing word here and there.

But in order for a piece of text to be legally considered your own creation, you have to have actually written it yourself. A human prompt that tells an AI to go off and create something is not considered copyrightable material.

This is actually very good news for creative and artistic industries because it means that there will always be a market and need for human ingenuity and creativity.

There's quite a bit of concern about AI in general, but I happen to think from a commercial content perspective, it probably won't change an awful lot in the next few years beyond how I've described it.

But AI-generated content is still going to continue to flood the internet, as it has for the past couple of years. It's going to become more sophisticated; it's also going to probably be used in questionable ways.

My concerns remain the same as always. AI can be used to create false and misleading content in order to convince people of a lie. I'm sure you can imagine all manner of ways in which such powerful and persuasive technology could be abused by bad-faith actors.

Imagine AI-generated video and audio being used to create false depictions of historical events and fabricated archival footage. AI can be used to generate fake recordings of public figures, politicians, and famous people.

I've already discussed the potential for it to be used to defame a person by making it look like they've said or done something that they haven't. This would all make it harder still for people to discern truth from illusion. Fact from fiction. That's certainly a sobering thought.

We're told the answer to this problem will be, somewhat ironically, AI-based AI detection tools. So, to identify AI-generated content, AI systems would be deployed. Sounds sensible, except we also have to take the AI detection tools' word for it. We have to take their assessment on faith. You see, my concern here is that the manipulation of information can swing both ways.

There are people who might create realistic AI-generated content to convince people of a lie, but also, there might be people in positions of authority who will claim that an AI detection tool has debunked a video as fake when it is, in fact, real. This could lead to the creation of false fact checks.

In a hypothetical scenario, you watch a video that appears to be completely convincing and authentic. Then, an AI detection tool proceeds to analyse it and claims that it's AI-generated and, therefore, fake. And that might be entirely true, or it might not.

How would you know the AI detection tool was correct? Could it be mistaken or, worse, programmed to lie? If we, the viewers, cannot verify the inner workings of the AI detection tool's coding, how can we be sure that it hasn't deceived us because the people who programmed it instructed it to?

As powerful and impressive as artificial intelligence systems are, I can't help but think that their invention has just created more hassle than their worth. I can think of a few new, groundbreaking technologies throughout history that have actually resulted in the creation of new problems and headaches for humanity to address.

We may look back at the normalising of AI in a few years and conclude that it seems to have come at quite a high price.

CHAPTER SIX

There was a time when I was a tech journalist, and I look back at that period of reviewing smartphones and laptops and new gadgets, and I kind of cringe a bit. I'm at a point now where I would love nothing more than to live in a time where I don't need modern consumer Internet-connected technology in my life every day. I feel this way especially because of its intrusiveness in our lives but also because, in the Western world, it's becoming increasingly difficult to live without it. I really resent that. I've become very nostalgic for the simpler times of the 1990s.

So many services we use have been digitised. If digital IDs and digital currencies become normalised, then essentially, your very ability to be a functioning citizen in society is contingent on conforming to them.

But should we not have the right to continue to live freely and contribute to society without the need to keep up with the latest technology trends?

The simplicity, speed, efficiency, and convenience offered by modern technology have made it so that a lot of consumer tech, such as Internet-connected devices, smartphones, etc, have become invaluable, ubiquitous, and indispensable. As a result, they become a bottleneck or a gateway to the rest of the world, which can, theoretically be controlled, of course.

So, this is why a business can, hypothetically make it

mandatory for you to use a QR code app on your phone to enter their store, enter a restaurant or football stadium, get on a plane, or other such form of transport.

As a result, I've come to see the dangers of technology more and more and the fact that its development is really going unchecked and unchallenged. A new product is launched by a big tech giant, and then we're told this is going to be the norm in the future. Anyone who resists change is considered to be a "dinosaur" who is "stuck in the past."

Given the absolute state of the world and where it's gone in recent years, I look back with increasing fondness at the past. And not just with some kind of sentimental, rose-tinted glasses. I'm glad to say that I am old enough to remember a time before the Internet, the slower pace and the less hectic nature of life. At least I experienced that time and can appreciate what we once had and could have again if we so chose.

The Internet was first made publicly available in 1993. At the time of writing this book, that was only 31 years ago. That's really not very long at all. Did we ever think the Web would become as indispensable and influential as it has?

It seems quite amusing to say this now, but there were many people at the time who thought the Internet wouldn't catch on and that it would fade away irrevocably after a few short years. This was because they figured that not enough people would purchase personal computers. However, the 1990s saw personal computers become far more affordable, powerful, and common.

In my home, we got our first proper Windows PC in 1997. I remember it had an Intel Pentium 1 processor with a clock speed of 200 MHz. It had just 16MB of RAM and a four-gigabyte hard drive. These specs were considered jaw-dropping at the time. We didn't get a functioning Internet connection until around 1998, but back then, computing was more of a hobbyist's interest. And I think that's why we appreciated it more. The Internet was a novelty and an exciting new place, accessible via an old 56kbp dial-up connection.

As slow, unstable, and sometimes challenging as those old PCs were back then, it was all new to us. It was fun to discover this new world of computing and all of its possibilities. Gaming, productivity, communication, networking, research, and entertainment - it was all developing at that point. But the potential for the world we now live in was always there.

But the Internet didn't die the death that some of its detractors thought it would. It grew and became a permanent and deeply ingrained part of our lives. Back in the late 90s, no one really thought it would become as indispensable as it did.

No one would have believed that so many businesses and services would move online, some of them exclusively. Fewer still would have believed that life without the Internet in some small fashion would become unthinkable. Was the Internet really meant to become as essential as it has? Was it designed from the beginning to be so?

Describing the Internet as a web seemed quite appropriate, given how inseparably entangled, dependent, and wedded to it we've become. I've grown to resent the Internet's omnipresence in our lives. I kind of wish we'd switch the bloody thing off from time to time and live without it for a while. It would probably be good for us to relearn how to live free from its ever-present influence at a slower pace of life. But that's a rather far-fetched notion at this point.

I would totally understand, Dear Reader, if you considered me to be a moany, crusty old man, shaking my fist at clouds. After all, they say there's no stopping so-called "progress."

I think the instantaneous nature of modern consumer tech has definitely caused an atomising effect. This is especially the case with smartphones and social media. Attention spans have been challenged, to say the least.

Even in the late 90s and early 2000s, to use the Internet required you to turn on a desktop computer in a room. So you couldn't always be connected and available online, now you're never off-line unless the phone, the tablet, the laptop is switched off. You're expected to be always within reach.

I think one of the most absurd new gimmick smart devices to come on the market in recent years is the smart speaker. I think it's totally absurd to have what are basically, in my view, surveillance devices in your home. They're basically listening devices that allow a faceless tech giant to hear what's going on in your home and intrude upon your privacy.

To voluntarily buy one of these and use it at home is just crazy, but I think it speaks to the shortsighted, novelty-seeking age we live in, where people just consume the new product that comes out without thinking things through. I'm absolutely astounded at how popular smart speakers have become and how much blind trust people place in them.

Augmented Reality Devices

So, I'll switch gears now and discuss augmented reality devices and the phenomenon of mixed-reality headsets. At the moment, such machines carry quite a high price tag, but their cost will come down as consumer demand increases and as the technology advances.

These things concern me because I think we have a big enough issue with people already being obsessively buried in their smartphones to an unhealthy degree. Do we really need them to now have a smart device physically strapped to their heads? I'm really hoping that we won't be seeing people walking down the street with these things stuck to their faces.

There's something immensely disturbing about VR and AR tech, in my opinion. I've used virtual reality before, as I'm sure many of you have. It can certainly be impressive, but it's the ultimate manifestation of how isolating and atomising technology can become. I find it very transhuman. It defaces the person quite literally, covering their eyes as they lose themselves in a total fantasy world, interacting with virtual screens and objects in their field of view that aren't actually there.

I think there's a significant spiritual lack in people, and the consumerist society we live in operates by taking advantage of this, trying to fill the emptiness in people. Many of these people work in corporate jobs that provide them with little to no satisfaction or meaning.

There's a young generation who can't afford to buy a home or start a family. They just feel life has no purpose. And it's very sad. But then consumer society tells them to seek meaning and distraction in retail therapy, materialism, frivolity, hedonism, another holiday, overpriced fancy clothes, and another overpriced smartphone.

The next novelty is a shiny new thing to briefly fill that void inside you until it wears off, and then it's on to the next consumer product. So many consumers and influencers are chasing the next gadget that seemingly promises to improve the quality of their lives and fill the emptiness inside them. But it never works. It's just an endless cycle of consumerism. I look at some of these people and see my past self. All this VR and augmented reality stuff just feels like a retreat into a pod life.

I think Man needs to seriously decouple from his over-reliance on consumer technology because it's driving him into an artificial, bug-man life. These devices are capturing his time, his mind and his focus inside unreal worlds and simulated environments. What does it say about us that we see the need to augment our perception of the world around us with digital phantoms?

The further Man descends into the technological and the virtual, the further he becomes disconnected from natural law and his own humanity. It's like he is receding from the real world, escaping into a fantasy, a dream world that he wishes to be the ultimate master of.

It ultimately won't provide the fulfilment and contentment that people are seeking. We cannot derive meaning from mere materialism. We are spiritual beings with needs beyond the physical.

I look upon these expensive AR glasses and headsets as nothing but cringeworthy luxury items. Our world is chock full of enough fakery and illusion as it is without compounding the issue further by embracing a hollow realm of immersive fantasy.

CHAPTER SEVEN

Technology is not the answer to everything.

The following is from a video essay I wrote back in 2015, which has been updated in 2025.

The Western world has become obsessed with discovering often needless consumer technology solutions to problems that either don't exist or that are being solved quite effectively through conventional means.

My conservatism regarding new technology is based primarily on the notion that moving humanity too far away from nature and making us dependent on artificial systems is detrimental to our survival.

Of course, I love what technology does for us, but I'm deeply concerned with what it can do *to* us and to our society. Breakthroughs in medical technology, advancements in aviation, transport, and communications, and the development of convenient domestic appliances have brought significant improvements to our lives.

Technological progress in these areas has delivered us from long commutes and time and labour-intensive work and made it possible to speak to people on the other side of the planet.

The Internet has provided knowledge and entertainment and given businesses new shop windows to reach their customers in entirely new ways. I have no problem with technology being an extensive force in human society; my problem is with it becoming too invasive. This was the reason that, for some time, I downgraded from a smartphone to a regular, old-school mobile phone. This was a decision I was forced to reverse, as I've previously mentioned. All I needed at the time was for my phone to enable me to make and receive calls and text messages.

When I got my first smartphone, way back in 2010, I found that anything beyond the most basic communications functions began to make me too busy and too occupied, too glued to the screen. Smartphones are devices that offer an insane amount of functionality; they are a camera, a web browser, a virtual social platform, and they provide us with email, gaming, a sat nav, and a multitude of other functions.

Unlike traditional phones that serve an immediate purpose, smartphones are designed to keep us engaged constantly. They addict us to them and keep obsessively dragging our attention back to social media posts, messages, updates, and the brainless games we play on them. They take us out of the moment and remove us from reality, damaging friendships and relationships and negatively impacting our attention spans.

My point is that we can benefit from technology enormously, but we don't need all of it all the time, and a smartphone is simply too many functions (some useful, some not) in one device. I think it's important for us to draw a line in the sand and determine how far we allow technology to encroach upon our lives.

Twenty years ago, no one would have believed you if you told them that they would willingly publicise personal online details about their careers and personal lives on a daily basis. In fact, it was only a few short years before social media emerged that the rule of thumb of Internet usage was to keep personal details as private as possible. It was just a good online habit to not divulge too much information about yourself to total strangers over the Internet. It was just good common sense and wisdom.

But, the sudden emergence of social networks in the early 2000s seemed to make people jettison this basic logical advice. People began to freely post their photos and their thoughts for all the world to see.

Moreover, the rise of the Internet of Things has indoctrinated us to believe that everyday household items and mundane inanimate objects, from toothbrushes, smart home appliances, wearables, and even light bulbs, are improved upon by being connected to the Internet.

There are literally apps built into toothbrushes that provide you with an online dashboard with graphs and charts offering detailed information about how to improve your brushing technique.

Need to lose weight? Get a device for your wristwatch that will track your steps and monitor your calories burned. Feeling too lazy to get out of your armchair and close the curtains? Use your smartphone to close your smart curtains for you. Heaven forfend if one had to actually shift their butt off the couch and manually open the curtains by hand. The horror. This is a form of infantilisation, in my opinion, the belief that human beings should allow technology to do everything for them. We want to be wrapped up in a self-centred bubble of technology that caters to our every whim.

There's a kind of cyclical problem at work here. As technology advances, we feel we become even more masterful of the world around us. The consumer technologies we wield every day give us more and more convenience, and soon, we become normalised to their daily presence and value.

As our technological sophistication increases, we fall into a kind of technology trap whereby our practical skills are greatly diminished. We become unable to live without our smartphones, our tablets, our wearables, our Wi-Fi, and our smart appliances.

My concern is what happens when these systems break down or go offline. People and businesses forget how they once functioned in the times before these technologies. Smartphones are like an extra limb to some people, just ask the majority of young millennials and Gen Zers today how they would plan to spend their time during a power cut, particularly when there's no means of recharging their devices.

Such situations, despite being a rare occurrence, truly demonstrate just how dominant technology is in our lives. These instances make it apparent that, in some respects, the technology itself is in charge of us.

I will provide you with three anecdotes that fully illustrate the point that I am making.

My sister called me once to tell me that she had a crippling virus on her smartphone. Think about this for a second. A smartphone is an appliance-like computing device with a mobile operating system far more simplified than that of a desktop computer.

In many respects, a smartphone is more personal a computer than an actual desktop or laptop PC. A person's entire life is on their phone. Their calendar, emails, contacts, web browsing bookmarks, credit card details, family photos, and a myriad of other personal details are all contained within this handheld machine. Yet, thanks to the significant advancements in mobile software of recent years, they have now become as prone to malware as conventional computers.

Given how dependent users are on their smartphones and how identity theft is rife nowadays, the idea that a virus could so easily commandeer control of a handset seems totally unacceptable. Yet about ten years ago, prior to the introduction and widespread adoption of smartphones, the idea that a person's old-school mobile cell phone could be compromised by a virus was not only unthinkable but practically impossible.

A simplistic little Nokia basic phone cannot be affected in this way. But smartphone users face life-disrupting inconveniences by such software corruption. It seems with each technical advancement of a consumer device; users enjoy more and more features and functions. But they come at a cost. That cost becomes immediately demonstrated as soon as something goes wrong. The higher we climb technologically, the farther society has to fall when it fails us.

My second example took place when I was on holiday some years ago. Myself and a friend walked into a bar in a hotel to find that the software used by the pub's cash registers had gone offline. None of the bar staff could take any orders for drinks or food. As a consequence, the bar was filled with some pretty unhappy patrons.

I remember remarking at the time that this is what happens when we embrace technology just a little too tightly. No member of staff could so much as pour a pint behind the bar because they couldn't take anyone's cash. Every transaction had to be registered through the online payment system they used. Flashback to pre-Internet-based cash register machines and the bar staff would have simply placed the order manually. This incident was truly frustrating because none of the bar staff knew what to do as soon as the technology stopped working. They just stood there like idiots behind the bar, clueless and confused.

I sat there wondering why they couldn't just revert to traditional manual payment calculations or use paper and pen to figure it out. They actually lost quite a bit of business that afternoon because of an inflexible, dogmatic adherence to modern technology and the inability to think beyond it.

I recognise that not all bars and pubs operate this way, but more and more of them will in time. In the future, customers of all manner of businesses will be required to own a smartphone and use NFC methods or QR codes to pay for things.

What happens when these systems fail, and no one has any experience making paper cash transactions? Does that mean that you simply shrug your shoulders and walk out of the grocery store with no food?

My final example is very similar. A family member was visiting the hospital once, and they needed to register at reception for their appointment with a consultant. I went with them, and we discovered that the hospital had installed self-service check-in kiosks. They looked and functioned somewhat similar to airport self-service machines. We were prompted by a receptionist to make use of one; the trouble is, they were all out of order.

Suffice it to say there were significant queues forming in the waiting area and some truly unhappy and frustrated patients waiting hours due to the inconvenience.

Plenty of apologies were made by reception, but no

real practical solutions were provided until such time as a technician had repaired one of the machines. By the time it came back online, there was an enormous queue snaking around the halls of the hospital to use it.

Why couldn't the reception staff simply revert to the original method of patient registrations? Simple pen and paper may create excess paperwork and bookkeeping, but it's bulletproof. It doesn't break down; it doesn't require software or electricity.

Sometimes, the best solutions are the simplest. The money spent on these unnecessary machines could have been invested where it was needed the most, on medical technology in the hospital or on hiring more nurses and staff.

I'm well aware that as I make this argument, I'm going to be misinterpreted by many people. I'll be told that I'm either being hypocritical or that I'm arguing that we should all go back and live in caves without modern medicine, clean drinking water, or central heating. This is a gross and, I would argue, intellectually dishonest oversimplification of my argument.

Man's ability to invent technological solutions to problems and improve our lives is what separates us from all other primates.

The problem I have with the rapid pace of consumer technology adoption is that it moves too far and too fast. It can make us dependent on an unsustainable system and rob us of skills we once had to achieve the same results. It can sometimes free up our time by doing laborious and time-consuming tasks much quicker. But with all the time and energy we save with one form of new technology, we seem to invent more distracting technologies to blow the time and energy we tried to save in the first place.

I don't think anyone should try to stand in the way of technological progress. However, the word progress suggests we are progressing toward something. If we fail to question where we're going, we'll wake up one day in the future unable to so much as tie our own shoelaces without having a device of some kind to do it for us.

By all means, let's continue to make technical advancements, but let's be mindful of where and how we focus our energies. We're all reliant on technology to various degrees, from cars to electricity to telephones and the Internet. But there's a balance to be achieved here.

The next generation will likely live in a world relying on more technology than we currently do. The generation after them will rely on yet more technology still.

Surely, our goal should be to educate ourselves as individuals with more practical and traditional skills so that we can adapt to emergency situations when technology fails us.

The reason I say this is because corporations and governments are never going to encourage the citizenry to develop true independence. They want us to depend on their products and the systems they create in order to protect their revenues and authority.

We must become intellectually and practically independent of machines that are designed to relieve us of certain skills.

I feel that the love of technological dependence our society has succumbed to is leading us down a path to stupidity and self-destruction.

CHAPTER EIGHT

AI Companionship and The Joi Effect

I'm simply blown away by the phenomenal acceleration in the development and proliferation of AI tools in just a few short years, especially since 2022. I think we're on the cusp of seeing some sci-fi-level personal assistants that will greatly surpass the ones on the market right now, by some orders of magnitude.

AI chatbots are advancing at an incredible rate, thanks to the machine learning capabilities of AI language models being used by millions of users every day. The next generation of virtual assistants will be fully interactive and highly sophisticated to the point of skirting the borders of self-awareness.

Imagine a virtual assistant helping to run and manage your daily life, a personal helper on your smartphone or smartwatch, much like Tony Stark's Jarvis. It will integrate with your connected home products. You'll be able to speak with these non-human virtual entities in completely natural conversation as you would with a real person.

You won't need to pull up a search engine on your phone and type in a search query anymore. You'll simply verbally ask your assistant any question, and its response will be based upon its near-immediate web search. It'll package the search results into a conversational response, collating the information in as concise or detailed a reply as you'd like. It'll serve as your personal shopper, making purchases for you online and only requiring your biometric authorisation to complete the transaction. It'll book the flights for your next trip, find a suitable hotel, and take care of every aspect of your itinerary if you so choose. They'll manage your finances, do your accounting, and file your tax returns.

Above all, these AI assistants will become indispensable daily companions, and the word companion is particularly critical to this topic. Increasingly, we're going to start seeing artificial, digital entities becoming the norm in everyday life in the coming years.

This reminds me of something Elon Musk said when he announced Tesla's Optimus Robots in October of 2024. He said, "It will basically do anything you want. It can be a teacher. It can babysit your kids, walk your dog, mow your lawn, get the groceries, just be your friend, and serve drinks. Whatever you can think of, it will do, and it's going to be awesome."

The bit in there about a robot being your friend is the thing that troubles me the most; the same goes for AI chatbots and digital entities. These things aren't real. They're not human, and yet, our experiences with conversing with them will feel frighteningly authentic.

Ultimately, my problem with the normalisation of relationships with artificial beings such as these is that developing such relationships only further serves to distance human beings from each other. This creates yet more potential for isolation, atomisation, and anti-social outcomes.

Why do I want to have a friendship with a machine when I can have a genuine friendship with a real, flesh-and-blood person? If anything, developing a connection with an AI is just keeping you from engaging with other humans.

Our modern smart tech and social media are keeping us atomised and anti-social enough as it is without robots, AIs, and androids, only worsening this problem. Yet, there's an inevitability about all of this, given how quickly the language models are learning. Certainly, within a few short years, the presence of robots in our towns and cities will become an everyday occurrence.

As their capabilities advance and their costs decline, they will only increase in numeracy. Initially, we'll see them work at the front desk of hotels, serve us coffee in cafes, offer directions in the subway, and scan and bag our groceries at the supermarket checkout.

The public will become quickly accustomed to engaging in conversation with such artificial "lifeforms" on a regular basis. Soon after, robots will begin accomplishing even more skilled labour, replacing humans in increasing areas of the workforce.

I can certainly foresee the police forces of the world being augmented by robot officers before too long, with all of the nightmarish dystopian possibilities such a scenario might entail.

There are those who say that robot workers will never be capable of replacing highly technical, skilled labour that requires fine motor control, improvisation, and complex problem-solving. I'm referring to trades like electrical engineering, plumbing, carpentry, DIY, infrastructural maintenance, building, and more. But I would argue these will merely be the last domains of human labour until sufficient advances are made in android and robot technologies are made. Keep in mind that AI systems with the capability of seeing the world around them will become even better at copying human actions through observation. They will learn not just through programming instructions, but by self-learning through copying humans.

With enough time and technical progress, every job done by a human can and likely will be eventually taken by a machine. It gives me no pleasure to say this, but it's just how I see the trajectory of automated technologies taking us.

If you're old enough to remember life before the Internet, then you can remember life before the smartphone and mobile phone. You can remember how transformative and society-changing these technologies were and how, in just a few short years, life was never the same again.

What's going to be the next consumer tech breakthrough that changes the world in a similar manner? I can tell you now it's not going to be VR or augmented reality. It's going to be the normalisation of non-human, artificial entities in our lives. Whether it's friendly chatbots speaking to us online or over the phone (instead of human call centre employees), robots serving us in restaurants or our own personal AI assistants managing our daily lives, the coming decades will be shaped by the rise of artificially intelligent robots and digital beings.

Humanity's relationship with smart technology has radically altered how we communicate, think, socialise, learn, and consume media. But the key word here is 'relationship.' People are going to be having relationships with these artificial beings. Your AI assistant will be like a close buddy. Elon Musk says your Optimus Robot can be your friend.

Imagine a future where robots, androids, and

digital assistants function as our daily companions. The idea of such technologies providing someone with companionship is hardly a far-fetched proposition, considering this is a topic covered numerous times in popular science fiction. I can even envisage people developing emotional connections to such systems.

Suppose future AIs boast their own believable personalities (which you will likely choose for them), and conversing with them becomes indistinguishable from conversing with another human being. In that case, emotional bonds between humans and machines become highly likely.

Some might even champion such artificial beings as the solution to the loneliness epidemic that's gripped a generation of young people across the West. The problem is that it doesn't actually solve the problem of loneliness or isolation, it merely compounds it by encouraging an individual to lose themselves in a one-sided relationship with a digital phantom.

A film that explores this topic quite brilliantly is the 2017 sci-fi movie Blade Runner 2049, the sequel to the 1982 cult classic. I won't go through a comprehensive plot breakdown because I merely want to focus on the protagonist of K, played by Ryan Gosling and his holographic companion named Joi, played by Ana de Armas.

K is a replicant, a biological machine, very much like a human but grown in a laboratory rather than born of a human mother. Joi appears to K in his home and later via a portable emanator through the use of holographic projection. She's intangible, meaning she has no physical body, K can't touch her.

Joi serves as his girlfriend, offering him a simulation

of a romantic relationship. She can even adapt her appearance and personality to his moods and desires.

During the course of the film, Joi offers K emotional support and appears to demonstrate genuine affection, care and concern for his well-being. At one point, during a particularly personal revelation for K, she even breaks down in holographic tears.

Later in the film (spoiler alert), Joi pleads for K's life while he is being physically beaten by the antagonist, Luv. Joi's final act appears to be a selfless one, she reactivates herself using the emanator, thus revealing her existence to Luv. Joi moves quickly to tell the wounded K that she loves him just before Luv cruelly stomps on the emanator, thus destroying Joi forever.

To many fans, Joi's actions here look like a demonstration of a deep and authentic love for K. Some argue that despite the fact that Joi is a convincing computer program developed by the Wallace Corporation, she must have evolved beyond her original programming. They theorise that Joi became more than a mere computer program. She asked K to transfer her program inside the emanator so that his pursuers could not download information from her program and locate K. This request could be interpreted as a very human-like self-preservation impulse but also a thoughtful consideration for K's life. They see this as evidence of her own free will.

However, there are other interpretations.

I think to explore this topic, we must first consider the point of K's journey in the story. K becomes convinced, for a time, that he may be born of a human mother. This belief transforms his perception of himself for some time, giving him a new sense of purpose and meaning.

Tragically, he discovers his memories of his

childhood are, in fact, not authentic. K is, indeed, a replicant and therefore, a product of the Wallace corporation, just as Joi is. The difference between them is that he is at least closer to being a real human than she is, given that he is biological in nature. He can genuinely feel real human emotions.

After Joi is destroyed, K later observes a giant holographic advertisement of the Joi product. It speaks directly to him, telling him that he "Looks lonely." She says she can "Fix that." She calls him a "Good Joe." Joe was the name his Joi had given him earlier in the film. The gigantic Joi hologram stares at K with lifeless, black eyes that lack any remote hint of humanity. The slogan on the billboard behind her reads, "Everything you want to see, everything you want to hear."

It's at this moment that K realises that his relationship with his Joi was built on a lie. Her affection for him, even her seemingly selfless concern, was nothing more than a sophisticated illusion. She was capable of simulating human emotions but couldn't actually experience them.

Joi was programmed with the ability to learn and to adapt to her user's needs. She could make choices within certain parameters but lacked the capability of defying her programming. She was ultimately designed to tell her user what they needed to hear in any given scenario.

The hologram was programmed to provide a completely convincing portrayal of romantic love, affection and companionship. There's no conscious agent behind that programming, no real thinking mind, just a series of predictive algorithms that can anticipate and adapt to the user's needs.

When K briefly believed he was a real human, his Joi

had described him as special. When he discovered the truth that he wasn't a real human, this raised his consciousness so that he could see Joi for what she truly was. He realised that there was nothing truly special about his relationship with Joi or her connection to him. He was just one of many millions of other Wallace Corp customers who naively believed that their Joi was unique and special and truly loved them.

In the end, K decides, of his own genuine free will, to defy his creators and experience something truly authentically human. He sacrifices himself for a greater purpose, thus proving that he is capable of something beyond his creator's original programming.

One of the primary themes of the Blade Runner story has always been about exploring what it means to be human.

I've heard arguments claiming that if a program like Joi is sufficiently convincing for her user, then that makes her real enough. In other words, if the user subjectively feels like Joi is a real woman, then she is real, and so too, is her love and affection.

The problem with this logic is that it denies objective reality. Compare this kind of thinking to Morpheous' warning in The Matrix. He asks Neo, "What is real? How do you define 'real'? If you're talking about what you can feel, what you can smell, what you can taste and see, then 'real' is simply electrical signals interpreted by your brain."

In The Matrix, the main characters are attempting to escape the convincing lie of the virtual world in order to discover the reality of the real world.

Conversely, the character of Cypher decides he cannot accept living in the hellish dystopia of reality and chooses to be placed back into The Matrix. He describes his virtual steak as juicy and delicious and believes that ignorance is bliss. He would rather he had no memory of the real world.

I think the people who argue for Joi being a self-aware and truly loving being are inadvertently taking Cypher's side in the reality argument.

Deciding to believe that Joi is real enough because of one's own subjective experience of her is a solipsistic interpretation of reality. But just like a simulation in The Matrix, we shouldn't be sufficiently satisfied that Joi *seems* real, we should actually want to know for sure if she truly *is* real.

Love is more than just feelings and emotions; it is many things; it is actions, it is the choices a person makes with regard to the object of their affection. But on a base level, to feel love, one needs to be capable of experiencing human feelings. This requires an actual biological nervous system that includes chemicals, hormones, etc, along with human sensory inputs that allow us to process real sensations and emotions.

A real human brain is essential to experiencing love, just as it is for any other emotion. If the amygdala senses danger, it sends signals to our heart to pump blood faster around our bodies, our heart rate increases, our adrenaline goes up, and we prepare to fight or flee.

Similarly, when we feel joy or sadness, signals from our brain's limbic system manifest in sensations in the heart. A flutter of happiness or soul-crushing heartbreak.

To act upon the feeling of love requires the physical, biological hardware to first experience the emotion. It requires free will for a person to act upon that feeling. Therefore, a mere computer program composed of algorithms and coding cannot truly love someone because it lacks all of the key components necessary to do so. It can, however, provide a convincing simulation of love but nothing more.

Objectively speaking, Joi cannot be real, and so her love, affection and concern for K cannot be real either because she does not possess the required human biology to feel and express emotion. She can technically offer him simulated affection, which he can subjectively internalise and interpret as love, and he can genuinely lavish love and affection upon her, but unlike him, she lacks the capability of receiving it.

This means the relationship is entirely one-sided. The only real flesh and blood person experiencing emotions in this scenario is K. He may believe that he is experiencing the presence and companionship of another person, but in truth, he is actually alone in his apartment with a human-shaped holographic program.

This is the central problem with non-human virtual entities, robots and AI companions. They do not and cannot provide authentic human relationships. These programs would be nothing more than emotional and spiritual parasites. They're like digital vampires draining your soul by consuming your love and affection and causing you to expend it on an object that cannot return your feelings. The entity is keeping you from connecting with a real flesh-and-blood human like yourself who is capable of feeling and perceiving the world as you do.

Such digital entities would be merely getting in the way of a person having an authentic and wholesome relationship with a real person, just as social networks keep a person from being genuinely social in the real world.

This is what truly bugs me about the idea of a future where people forge friendships and connections with machines. Social media has undermined what the word 'friend' actually means. Before certain social networks, a friend was someone you were actually on friendly terms with, nowadays, a friend is merely someone you've accepted a friend request from. It devalues the very idea of friendship. Likewise, a robot or AI cannot be your friend any more than your smartphone can be your friend.

Despite my thoughts on this issue, I nevertheless foresee a future where a certain percentage of the population will engage in friendships and relationships with artificial entities. The reason I see this happening is due to the recent arc of consumer technology over the past twenty years.

We've seen that if it's possible for big tech to introduce a particular kind of consumer product, it will be created, and it will be mass-marketed. This has been the way of things for a long time now. If something *can* be built, it *will* be built without so much as a momentary consideration of the potential negative and or harmful consequences of its introduction.

Look how transformative touchscreen smartphones were after they were introduced. We quickly saw the emergence of the smartphone zombie, a person who walks down the street with their head buried in their device, without any awareness of the world around them. Social settings and face-to-face conversations are intruded on by the constant addictive tug of notifications and social media messages.

Live music events such as concerts have never been the same now that crowds are filled with people filming the entire event on their phones rather than actually experiencing it first-hand through their own eyes. Apparently, everything has to be filmed and recorded, or it never happened.

Smartphones have made people less present in the real world and negatively impacted attention spans, but they're not going anywhere. I see no reason why a similarly negative cultural and societal transformation won't take place following the advent and normalisation of non-human virtual entities, robots and AI companions.

Humanity appears to be stupid enough to adopt any new-fangled consumer tech without so much as a consideration for the long-term consequences at a personal or societal level.

While a person could feel genuine fondness for their digital friend, they would need to be aware that such feelings cannot be reciprocated. Therefore, the robot or AI cannot truly empathise with them.

Furthermore, if young men do begin to enter into relationships with virtual girlfriends, it could potentially lead to other unforeseen negative outcomes.

For starters, the AI girlfriend requires zero effort to attract, so a man doesn't have to better himself, look after his physical fitness or work on his shortcomings in order to get one. He doesn't have to do any of the things he'd need to do to attract a real human woman. Without the adversity of competition with other males, personal stagnation is inevitable.

Needless to say, a digital girlfriend is a genetic dead end, offering no chance for reproduction. If a man is romantically placated by a digital girlfriend, it's no different to him being placated by pornography. The outcome is the same: no offspring and a lot of time wasted on a digital fantasy. This issue alone could have wider negative implications for civilisation itself.

Ultimately, relationships and friendships with

artificial beings merely create unsatisfying social experiences and a loss of meaning in life. They might trick the user into believing they're not actually alone, but in truth, they are. They also encourage further retreat into one's personal sanctum of the home, further distancing humans from each other. Unlike smartphones before them, perhaps legitimate concerns about friendships with non-human virtual entities can be raised and addressed before their normalisation.

CHAPTER NINE

When I was a kid, I remember my Mother talking about her favourite television presenters from her era. Men who did more than just present a TV show and who were multitalented and versatile. They could sing, dance, tell jokes with great comedic timing, and even do some acting. They were Jacks of all trades but highly competent at all of them.

It was a different time. To get on television and host a popular TV show, you needed talent and to be a variety performer. Nowadays, a TV presenter just needs to look physically attractive and reasonably able to read off a teleprompter.

Of course, there are exceptions, presenters with a few more skills to their repertoire, but by and large, TV presenting isn't what it used to be. My Father was also a man of many talents. He was a plumber by trade but highly knowledgeable in other fields, too. He could turn his hand to anything; he could do a bit of carpentry, welding, electrical work, and building.

To this day, I'm still astounded at the level of skill and capability he developed during his working life. I'm embarrassed to say that I don't have a tenth of his capabilities.

It might sound strange for me to say this, but one of

my biggest regrets in life is finishing school. In the summer before my final year of secondary school, I got a job working in a bank. I would later come to loath corporate jobs, but as a young man of 18 years of age, I didn't know any better at the time. I just enjoyed the novelty of it all and the freedom that earning my own money could afford me.

Above all, I was being given responsibilities I enjoyed while also being treated like an adult for a change. A far cry from the school environment.

I remember in late August of 2001, I went to my Mother and told her that I wanted to keep working and didn't want to return to school to complete my final year. I remember her reaction. She wasn't pleased about it, but I could tell she wasn't going to fight me hard on the issue either.

I know that my parents would have allowed me to leave school and stay at work if I'd really pushed. I would have also avoided the dreaded Leaving Certificate Examination, which is the final exit exam, end-level boss, and Earth-shattering showdown that every Irish student is supposed to endure.

I never learned anything of use in school. I don't remember the vast majority of what I was taught. I don't remember all of the English poetry. I don't remember any of the Irish poems or stories.

Irish is so poorly taught in schools that despite receiving 14 years of Irish lessons, I still can't speak the language. I barely remember any of the German I studied. I remember even less of the History, and the only thing I recall from the Geography class is something about oxbow lakes, which is to say, I can recall the words, "oxbow lake." I don't actually remember what they were or what looked like or anything.

As for Mathematics class, the less said about that, the better. Beyond basic addition, subtraction, multiplication, and division, I struggled badly at Maths. Seriously, why do they teach quadratic equations in school? What am I ever going to use them for?

I hated every moment of Maths to the point where I found it mentally agonising and highly stressful, probably because one of the Maths teachers I had was a deeply unlikeable, shouty, angry woman who just traumatised me.

The only subject I liked was English class, but more specifically, creative writing. I liked writing essays and telling stories. So, it came as a great disappointment to me to discover in my final year of school that we'd hardly write any essays at all. Most of the English curriculum that year focused on us being told by our English teacher what to think about a Shakespeare play or some depressing poem by Emily Dickinson.

We were then expected to reproduce what the teacher had explained in our own words but with no real intellectual deviation. This felt like a mindless process of accepting a particular point of view that isn't your own, absorbing large amounts of information, and then reproducing it. This appears to be how quite a lot of the education system operates.

This system isn't designed to produce a generation of intellectually curious, critical thinkers. It's designed to train and condition young adults for blind obedience to authority in later life. It's designed to produce a person who consumes slogans, propaganda and media messages, believes them, and repeats them without question. Garbage in, garbage out.

Suffice it to say, I caved to the fear of missing out on having a Leaving Cert. I was afraid that not doing the exam would hinder me in later life. Maybe it would have in the short term, but in the long term, I would have been far better off.

I wish I'd been a little bit braver and stuck to my guns. But I decided to listen to the voice of fear, nagging at the back of my mind.

Before I continue further, I don't mean to encourage any young people to drop out of secondary school. I merely have my own hangups with the system and wish I could have escaped it a year earlier. I would have much preferred to have been homeschooled.

I returned to school for my final year in September of 2001. The year was hell. I struggled with my revision for the year, primarily because I already knew what I wanted to do after I left school and felt like I had no reason or driving need to be there.

In the weeks before I returned to school, and just before I started working in the bank, I'd done a week-long video editing course. I loved it. I wanted to be a video editor or at least work in post-production in the film or television industry. I was also messing around with video editors on my home PC and making silly home movies, so I was learning the skills I needed. Skills that I would never develop in school.

The final year was long, stressful, and filled with anxieties, but I got through it. I somehow fumbled my way through the Leaving Cert examinations in the summer of 2002. I knew I'd done poorly, and my worries would be confirmed later that summer when the results were revealed. I'd passed, but only barely.

The good news is, it didn't matter that I did so poorly in the Leaving Cert. It actually didn't matter that I didn't remember the vast majority of my primary and secondary-level education. Because I'd never need any of it after I left school, none of it would be any benefit to my future jobs or, indeed, my final career as a journalist and video content creator. What a damning indictment of the education system.

All of the skills that I learned as part of my career, I taught myself through practice and playing around on my computer. Which just goes to show how utterly redundant the school system was for me.

Having said that, the school system can be very useful for those looking to pursue a career in teaching, which feels like a closed-loop ecosystem in a way. You learn all this proprietary information, which is of no real value in later life unless you intend to teach it to others. What's the point of that?

As an aside, given the actual state of modern education at this point and some of the completely inappropriate things being taught in schools, I've become a staunch advocate of homeschooling.

Now for the bad news. The Leaving Cert left a psychological scar. I'm 41 now. To this day, whenever I'm going through a particularly stressful time in my life, I still have dreams where I'm back in school for some reason, and I'm studying for my Leaving Cert and struggling to revise. Then, at some point in the dream, I put my hand up in class and tell the teacher I don't need to do this because I've already done the Leaving Cert. The dream ends.

This nightmare follows the exact same pattern every time. Visuals can differ, but the narrative is always the same. I've lost count of the number of times I've had this dream over the past twenty-two years of my life.

I did some research into this, and it turns out I'm not alone. Apparently, a lot of people report suffering from this very same recurring dream and tend to laugh it off as just one of those quirks of life. Just a normal, residual hangover from the right of passage of leaving school, growing up, and becoming an adult. In reality, it's an actual trauma and the mind's way of showing us that something is profoundly wrong with the school system and how we treat children and young adults.

I think schools do more harm than good. I actually believe they break the human soul and function like conformity factories that mass-produce compliant adults. People then enter the workforce and are already accustomed to the daily routine of repetitive, structured, institutional work. I think it's this education system that prepares people for the mind-numbing drudgery of the corporate wage-slave world.

In hindsight, I can think of another reason to have dropped out of school. I wish I'd gone into the trades. There may have been a lot of repetitive, unskilled, manual labour that robots have been able to replace in recent years, but specialised skilled trades like carpentry, plumbing, mechanical and electrical engineering, construction and ironwork are still some ways away from being taken over by robots.

A lot of my generation was encouraged to go into air-conditioned office work and sit in front of computers for a living. The explosion of the IT industry completely transformed the labour force. The vast majority of today's IT jobs didn't even exist twenty years ago. But the irony is that a lot of repetitive white-collar roles will be replaced by artificial intelligence. Not all of them, but quite a lot.

I suspect data entry, analytical work, translators, basic coding, and basic graphic design work will be greatly affected by AI. Skilled, specialised trade jobs will likely be safe from the advancement of automation for a while yet. But like I've said, the robots will come for those one day in the future.

This all got me thinking about the advancement of automation in the labour force. Specifically how we've come to accept the idea of being made redundant by machines in order to enrich the financial interests of big businesses.

Of course, technology can help to emancipate us from time and labour-intensive work, but there has to be a reasonability to this.

At a certain point, technology stops being a means of shortcutting tasks or providing us with more free time and value and begins to encroach upon our very reason for being. If automation continues to advance, both in terms of AI and robotics, then perhaps eventually, there will be no reason for Man to work at all. No requirement for Man's mental ingenuity, creativity, or physical capabilities. And then what?

What purpose do we have left as a species if we no longer have a purpose in life? This is why I complain so much about the unchecked advancement of modern technology. If it is let follow its inevitable course, it could result in the obsolescence of humanity.

Considering human beings have to continuously retrain and reinvent themselves every few years in order to adapt to the changes in advancing technologies, we have to ask, are we really in the driving seat of our own destiny? Or is the technology determining our fate?

At the same time, there are plenty of soul-destroying jobs I would not have any issue with seeing the end of.

Believe it or not, there is one thing that I agree with Karl Marx about, just one. This is his comment on modern industrial work, which is that industrial labour can be alienating because the worker is detached from the products of his labour. Of course, he was talking about factory work, but I think this could be applied even more so to the corporate office world.

I wanted to touch upon the corporate world and the rat race that so many people are still trapped within. Now, I'm not trying to compare careers or job types per se, just focusing on how man's work has changed and become less human-focused and, therefore, alienating and lacking in meaning and spiritual fulfilment.

If you're getting up in the morning at a ridiculously early hour to commute to a job you despise that provides little to no meaning for you, and you're in an emotionally draining, soul-destroying corporate office environment filled with bureaucracy, ask yourself why you're doing this?

Maybe you're clocking in like a corporate drone, doing mind-numbing repetitive work on a computer and carefully watching the clock, praying for five o'clock to roll around. If you're answering phones, doing sales, customer support, or even designing software, whatever it might be, you're not directly connected to the human element of your labour.

Consider your work life if you were living many decades ago in a small village, and you were a butcher, baker, hairdresser, or greengrocer. Someone at the centre of the community. You're in direct, real-world, face-to-face communication with your customers, and you're essentially a pillar of that place, you're an institution. You would be an important node for people in that community, and your work would have meaning and value beyond the mere labour itself.

You would be in direct social engagement and

contact with other human beings. But if you're in a corporate office cubicle speaking on the phone to a faceless customer or client about a complaint or a product or service - everything is very abstract, everything is virtual, unreal, cerebral, and removed from the human element. The product, service, and even the customer all become non-physical, reduced to being concepts of the mind.

When your boss brings you into the office for your monthly or quarterly performance review, the results of the quality of your work may be displayed in some kind of graph or numbers on a spreadsheet. This is how you're supposed to derive meaning and satisfaction from your hard work, but compare this to receiving a warm smile and kind words from a happy customer in your hypothetical greengrocer or bakery.

Even receiving a generous bonus in your pay packet for a job well done is ultimately only numbers in your bank balance displayed on a screen. And while the extra money might be very welcome to you that month, there's something cold and dislocated about how people work and earn money in a corporate environment that just doesn't speak to a deeper human need.

When I did this kind of work in these corporate environments, I recall feeling like an ant, a corporate worker bee. Everything about that world is designed to extract as much monetary value and profit from the individual as possible. You really feel like just a battery-farmed unit. And the emptiness of that life is only worsened by the difficult economic situation at the moment.

You roll out of bed at some ridiculously early hour. You then face a demoralising commute, and you sit in a small cubicle and do uninspiring work for most of the day until you get home and have a pitiful few hours of free time before you must repeat the process the following day. Throw in the high cost of living and how hard it is to own one's own property and pay bills, and it's a profoundly unsatisfying existence.

When corporations seek cheaper labour from abroad to replace their workforce, it's essentially a taste of what's to come, when the day finally arrives when robots can do everything humans can do.

So, technology has us do these soulless, air-conditioned computer-based office jobs, but ironically, further advancements in AI and automation technologies will take them away. How odd, indeed.

Transhumanism

This leads us inevitably to the topic of Transhumanism. The nightmare future at the end of the slippery slope of robotics and automation.

There was a naive time many years ago before we knew how big tech companies worked and what they stood for when the idea of a self-driving car was a really cool sci-fi concept. Who wouldn't want a car with an autopilot function? You could have a few beers, and then your self-driving car could drive you home. Sounds great, or rather, it did once upon a time. Not so much now.

Today, I'd be concerned that my self-driving car could be hacked and controlled by someone else. Or that it mightn't start at all if the company that makes it believes I've said something they deem "offensive" online. No doubt, the car would be recording my movements, and a tyrannical government would be able to track and surveil me wherever I drive.

Sci-fi movies and TV shows sold us the magical

dream of a utopian tech future, but the reality is something quite different. The same will likely be true with Transhumanism.

Wouldn't it be cool to have some brain chip in your head that lets you surf the Internet without a phone? A neural device that basically gives you superpowers. You could live in an augmented reality, interacting with a virtual world from within your own head. You could control computer interfaces with your mind.

Imagine being able to learn how to play an instrument or speak any language you wanted by just downloading the skills and knowledge directly into your brain. You'd have an encyclopedic knowledge of any topic. You would be a superior human being. An advanced being, made possible by such a technological evolution. Right? Maybe not.

Colour me sceptical, but it's more likely that transhumanism is just another means of money-hungry elites creating a more advanced robotic slave. One with the benefits of human abilities and attributes but with a few additional tech enhancements.

If you're ever worried about your computer or smartphone being hacked and having someone listen in on you, imagine how much worse life would be if the technology inside your body could be hacked in a similar manner. Could a person literally hear your thoughts? Could they possibly hack your bodily functions or even take control of you?

If a neural interface in our brain is capable of downloading information, what would stop a hacker from hiding a trojan or piece of malware in there? Could a person's brain crash like a computer? Could a person be turned into a cyborg zombie, losing control of their body and mind? Would you actually be surprised if such a thing were possible?

Transhumanism may be sold to people as some pathway to building a better human being and a gloriously utopian world, but the end result will likely be something hideously disturbing.

Transhumanists might make claims about how humans are just biological machines, but this isn't the case. We are divine beings made in the image of God, with a soul and will of our own. We are not broken, and we are not in need of cyborg "enhancement" or being "upgraded." We are already exactly as we are intended to be.

The Transhuman dream is simply about creating a better human mule or workhorse. A more efficient worker drone, and wage slave. And this is really a crucial aspect of this conversation.

What is Man truly attempting to achieve with endless, unchecked technological advancement? He started with simple tools for hunting and fishing. Before too long, he was farming and using a horse-drawn plough. A few centuries later, he's driving a car, flying around the world on aircraft, microwaving his meals, watching TV, and asking AI to write poetry for him.

The technology was a means of serving Man. So, why then, must we even consider entering a future where there will be nothing left for Man to do at all? No toil for him to seek satisfaction in. No rewarding challenge of labour to overcome and find purpose.

Is Man's fate to simply sit around and be waited on hand and foot by robot servants and to be amused by unending virtual entertainment created by machines?

A life of endless hedonism, frivolity, and leisure may sound fun for a time, but it would probably have the same soul-crushing effect of a boring office job before too long. It would offer man no new horizon to strive for or destiny to fulfil.

Technology should offer convenience, not enslavement. The closer man remains to nature, the closer he stays in touch with his humanity, the more fulfilling and meaningful his life and work will be.

To be close to nature is a spiritual act and an interface with God and the divine. The reason people are depressed and utterly lacking in meaning in their horrendous corporate workplace is because everything about that lifestyle and that world is lacking in everything Man needs to be happy. And the more advanced tech and AIs that you throw into the mix, the worse it'll become.

We have to ask ourselves, what is it we're trying to attain with our unabated technological progress? Is this progress taking us further or closer to a sense of peace, contentedness, and completion as individuals and as a species? I don't believe it is.

Therefore, we must ask the question: Can Man be satisfied with simply accepting living with a certain level of technological capacity and progressing no further? Because it seems to me that we're creating more problems for ourselves with our continuous advancements.

Humanity has always instinctively known the path to meaning and fulfilment, but like the arc of technological development itself, at some point, we got lost along the way. It's time to rediscover the road home.

CHAPTER TEN

The Loss of Hinterland

While technology has allowed man to conquer and tame his environment, simplify his life and automate enormous amounts of labour, there has been another depressing drawback. Global telecommunications systems have encapsulated practically every corner of the planet in an invisible digital web from which there is no escape.

No matter how far off the grid you try to flee to, no matter how remote you think you can get; from the highest mountain to the most barren desert or deepest forest, the Internet is everywhere, or near enough everywhere.

With further developments in satellite internet technologies, there will soon be no corner of the world where you won't have a web and or cellular connection on your phone. I can't stand the idea that there's nowhere I can go where I can't be reached by a phone call or text message, let alone a social media notification or location-tracking app on my phone.

Of course, some will celebrate this engineering achievement or be baffled by why I would even consider this to be a negative thing. Isn't having web access anywhere in the world a benefit? If someone gets into trouble in a remote place, they can contact someone on their smartphone for help. If you get lost somewhere, you can quickly find your way again by consulting an online mapping service or GPS. So where's the downside?

On the 23rd of December 2024, Elon Musk posted on X about his Starlink technology: "You can even have high-speed on a remote mountain in Antarctica!" My friend Morgoth's Review replied, "One of the most depressing sentences I've ever read."

I wholeheartedly agree with Morgoth's sentiments.

There is something truly saddening about the encroachment of technology into every inch of the natural world, spreading the tentacles of the Internet to even the most isolated of places. There's essentially nowhere on Earth a person can escape from the global telecommunications matrix.

While some might simply reply, "If you don't want to use the Internet when you're out rambling in the woods, hiking a mountain or fishing in a lake, just switch your phone off or leave it at home." I think this misses the point.

As Morgoth has mentioned, of course, you could choose to deactivate your smartphone or leave it at home, but this is an admission that smart technology has become such an intrusive force in our reality that it has essentially become the default state of being. Man is now required to intentionally and consciously opt out of being part of the online world, which has become the de facto norm.

The issue I have with this is that we've lost the romanticism that comes with the idea of a hinterland, a place far away from civilisation where a person can be detached and even lost. Yes, being lost and cut off from the world is desirable to some, even if it brings with it its own challenges or even dangers.

Total and complete blanket Wi-Fi coverage means that there is no remaining pocket of the world that hasn't been reached, catalogued and assimilated by the web and by extension, there's nowhere a potential authoritarian mass surveillance state cannot encroach upon if it so chooses.

I think, on some level, no matter how civilised and sophisticated we become, there's still something within us that innately yearns for the thrill of the wild, untamed and unknown. It's a component of the human soul and part of our desire for freedom.

But the relentless march of our technological advancement means that nothing appears to be sacred and there's nowhere we can be assured of privacy. All that appears to be left of the very concept of a hinterland is the privacy inside our minds, the thoughts in our heads.

However, even future smart tech aims to conquer the final frontier of our grey matter, with the forthcoming neural brain chips, for those who are foolish enough to consent to such fresh, dystopian hell.

The Unending Work Day: Loss of Work / Life Boundaries

About twenty years ago, I began to take notice of the intrusive nature of the early, pre-touchscreen smartphones. A problem that only dramatically worsened with the advent of the touchscreen smartphone. Suddenly, the corporate world was subtly placing more demands upon the time of its workers.

Because these mobile devices allowed a user to be always connected to the office via email, the boundaries between work life and home life began to break down.

The average corporate office worker was now tethered to the workplace in an unprecedented manner. I was never someone who accepted such a situation during my time in the corporate world, but there were plenty of brown-nosers who did.

From the moment they got out of bed and during their train or bus commute to the office, they had already begun their working day, answering emails an hour or two before they'd reached their desks. The power of web-connected, mobile devices had made these people even busier than they'd been before.

I do acknowledge the exception to this situation is people who are actually being paid to be on call. I'm specifically referring to those office workers who aren't getting paid to work out of their agreed hours.

While they may have thought that dialling into work a little earlier and answering a few emails was helping to give them a head start on their workday, they were actually shooting themselves in the foot without realising it.

The issue with this workaholic behaviour is that it has become the new normal to the point where your boss eventually expects it from you. To make matters worse, you're actually working for your employer outside of your contracted hours, and you're therefore not getting paid for this extra work.

You might think that answering a few work emails or working on a spreadsheet on the train is helping you catch up on your workload backlog and get ahead of your 9 am deadlines, but in actuality, you're only making things worse for yourself.

The more work you get done, the more work you'll be expected to do by your boss. Your smartphone and laptop are helping you be more productive, and the nature of profit-driven corporate wage slave work is all about increasing productivity and maximising output. Therefore, the more work the technology enables you to take on, the more work you'll be *required* to take on. This is the reason why it's become the norm for people to take work calls out of hours and remotely connect to work in the evening when they get home.

The issue is that your clients and customers also have smartphones and laptops and they too are now connecting to work before official office hours. So now, some people find themselves working longer hours without extra pay, thanks to the "convenience" of Internet-connected smartphones, tablets and laptops. Hurray for progress!

Taking Back What Smart Tech Stole From Us

It was around the time that touchscreen smartphones became common circa 2010 or so that there was a massive rise in the number of people seeking out mindfulness meditation videos and books.

For the first time, millions of people could now carry the Internet with them in their pockets, always connected. The Internet was no longer something that was accessible only from within the confines of a room in one's home; it was suddenly on demand, everywhere and anywhere.

Millions of smartphone-addicted users are trying to slow down their over-active minds, which have been overtaxed, overstimulated and bombarded by dopamine hits and endless content consumption and novelty. At a certain point, you have to ask yourself if your smartphone is making you more productive or just keeping you busy and distracted.

A lot of people are beginning to wake up to the realisation that their relationship with smart tech is simply unhealthy and born out of habit, addiction and a lack of self-discipline. They're also starting to realise how such smart technology doesn't necessarily improve the quality of their lives or add significant value.

Social media, especially, can serve as little more than a time suck or a source of stress, given the dizzying amount of content to consume and the negativity it can cultivate.

I acknowledge that some people need a smartphone and social media for work purposes. But for those people who don't necessarily need a smartphone and who wish to reduce the intrusiveness of smart tech in their lives, here are a few helpful tips.

1. Consider getting rid of your smartphone and downgrading to a regular, old-school dumb phone that has no Internet capability.

Note: Some basic feature phones have web browsers, email apps and even simplified versions of some social networks, but the experience of using them is so clunky and cumbersome that you're unlikely to use them with the same frequency as you would on a smartphone. It's a good way of disincentivizing compulsive Internet and social media usage.

2. If you still need to have a smartphone for whatever reason, consider leaving it at home or switching it off when you're outside. It's perfectly reasonable to want to sometimes be uncontactable and to indulge in some peace and quiet time.

3. Make a conscious effort to buy with cash in shops rather than tapping with your smartphone or bank card.

Note: A cashless society with programmable digital money and all of the controls that come with it will be impossible for governments to implement if people refuse to adopt smart tech systems. This is why keeping cash in circulation is very important.

4. Take stock of how much time you spend in front of a computer screen every day. Try to limit your screen time to the bare minimum or what is absolutely essential.

5. Try to take one day off the Internet each week, perhaps on a weekend.

6. Consider eliminating social media from your life entirely. For some people, this seems like a drastic step, but you'd be surprised how much you won't miss any of these apps after just a few days without them. You'll probably feel like a weight has been lifted. You'll have much more time to think and concentrate without all of the distracting notifications, updates and pointless feed scrolling that comes with regular social media usage.

Of course, this might mean you won't be in contact with certain people as often, so make an extended effort to keep in touch with them through conventional means like phone calls.

7. I think it should go without saying that you should make a greater effort to spend more time in the great outdoors. Thanks to smart tech, video games and streaming TV services, we've got practically unlimited entertainment and justification for staying indoors and living a fairly sedentary lifestyle. This is another habit for us to kick.

Getting out, being genuinely social in the real world and maintaining our physical health is of paramount importance.

AFTERWORD

I'd like to thank you for taking the time to finish reading this book. I truly hope you enjoyed reading it as much as I did writing it.

As an independent author, I need your help to promote my work. I'd really appreciate it if you could leave a review of *The Checkmate Machine* online and tell your friends and family about this book.

Please follow me at the links below:

Subscribe on YouTube.com/@TheDaveCullenShow Website: https://www.thedavecullenshow.com

Best wishes to you.

Dave Cullen

FOLLOW ME ON SOCIAL MEDIA

For regular updates about my work and video content, follow me on these platforms:

x.com/DaveCullenShow

gab.com/DaveCullen

minds.com/DaveCullen

ABOUT THE AUTHOR

Dave Cullen is an Irish journalist, author, and film critic. He is best known for his pop culture analysis and film and television reviews on his YouTube channel: The Dave Cullen Show.

youtube.com/@TheDaveCullenShow

OTHER BOOKS BY DAVE CULLEN

Deus v Machina: A Cody Stockton Mystery

Las Vegas, 2045. Beneath the sparkling neon-filled oasis of Sin City in the heart of the Nevada desert lurks a powerful evil force with a malevolent agenda. A seemingly accidental death turns out to be murder, exposing a shocking cover-up and a deadly Satanic cult. Private Investigator Cody Stockton uncovers a tangled web of corruption and lies that lead him to the heart of a global conspiracy. An advanced artificial intelligence with a will of its own and plans for world domination is about to collide with a man claiming to be the Son of God.

In a battle between the technological and the spiritual, Stockton's convictions are challenged and his faith shaken as he races to unravel the truth and save humanity. But in a war that was never meant for mere mortals, can one man really make a difference? **Available now from online bookstores in eBook, Paperback and Audiobook formats.**

www.ingramcontent.com/pod-product-compliance
Lightning Source LLC
LaVergne TN
LVHW051709050326
832903LV00032B/4100